PENGUIN BOOKS

FIRST AID FOR DOGS

Bruce Fogle, DVM, runs a veterinary practice in London and is a founding manager of the Emergency Veterinary Clinic, London, the first facility of its kind in Britain. He is the author of more than twenty books on pet care, including *The Complete Dog Care Manual* and *The Complete Dog Training Manual* and is a regular columnist for *The Daily Telegraph.*

D1019210

First Aid for DOGS

WHAT TO DO WHEN EMERGENCIES HAPPEN

Bruce Fogle

DVM

Illustrated by Amanda Williams

PENGUIN BOOKS

PENGUIN BOOKS
Published by the Penguin Group
Penguin Group (USA) Inc., 375 Hudson Street, New York, New York 10014, U.S.A.
Penguin Group (Canada), 90 Eglinton Avenue East, Suite 700, Toronto, Ontario, Canada M4P 2Y3 (a division of Pearson Penguin Canada Inc.)
Penguin Books Ltd, 80 Strand, London WC2R 0RL, England
Penguin Ireland, 25 St Stephen's Green, Dublin 2, Ireland (a division of Penguin Books Ltd)
Penguin Group (Australia), 250 Camberwell Road, Camberwell, Victoria 3124, Australia (a division of Pearson Australia Group Pty Ltd)
Penguin Books India Pvt Ltd, 11 Community Centre, Panchsheel Park, New Delhi – 110 017, India
Penguin Group (NZ), 67 Apollo Drive, Rosedale, North Shore, Auckland 0745, New Zealand (a division of Pearson New Zealand Ltd)
Penguin Books (South Africa) (Pty) Ltd, 24 Sturdee Avenue, Rosebank, Johannesburg 2196, South Africa

Penguin Books Ltd, Registered Offices: 80 Strand, London WC2R 0RL, England

First published in Penguin Books (U.K.) 1995
Published in Penguin Books (U.S.A.) 1997

13 15 17 19 20 18 16 14

Copyright © Bruce Fogle, 1995
Illustrations copyright © Amanda Williams, 1995
All rights reserved

LIBRARY OF CONGRESS CATALOGING IN PUBLICATION DATA
Fogle, Bruce.
First aid for dogs: what to do when emergencies happen/Bruce Fogle; illustrated by Amanda Williams.
p. cm.
Originally published: London: Pelham Books, 1995.
Includes index.
ISBN 978-0-14-025541-6
1. Dogs—Wounds and injuries—Treatment. 2. Dogs—Diseases—Treatment. 3. Veterinary emergencies. 4. First aid for animals. I. Title.
SF991.F574 1997
636.7'0896025—dc20 96-34004

Printed in the United States of America
Set in 11 ½ / 12 ½ pt Palatino

Except in the United States of America, this book is sold subject to the condition that it shall not, by way of trade or otherwise, be lent, resold, hired out, or otherwise circulated without the publisher's prior consent in any form of binding or cover other than that in which it is published and without a similar condition including this condition being imposed on the subsequent purchaser.

The scanning, uploading and distribution of this book via the Internet or via any other means without the permission of the publisher is illegal and punishable by law. Please purchase only authorized electronic editions, and do not participate in or encourage electronic piracy of copyrighted materials. Your support of the author's rights is appreciated.

Contents

Introduction

Dogs are living longer than ever before, and for logical reasons: routine inoculations have brought infectious diseases under good control; nutrition has improved; and we dog owners have a better understanding of our responsibilities, both to our pets and to our neighbours. Responsible ownership, simply controlling where our dogs go and what they do by walking them on leads, is perhaps the single most important factor in increased life expectancy. And what an increased life span it is! When I was a child a dog's life expectancy was about ten years. Today it ranges from thirteen to seventeen years, depending on size and breed of your canine. That is an amazing increase.

Most dog owners do not question whether good veterinary attention is nearby. That fact is taken for granted. What does puzzle or even worry owners is whether their pet's problem justifies the time and expense involved in a visit to the vet. As well as describing what to do when emergencies happen, this book advises on whether, and when, to seek a vet's help.

The book is divided into four parts. Part One describes what to do first when an emergency happens; how to restrain a dog, check its vital signs, maintain life, apply bandages and splints and safely transport the dog. Practice the instructions in this section as you read them, while your dog is robust and healthy. Understanding this section will enable you to act efficiently and knowledgeably in an emergency.

Part Two explains, step by step, what to do when the immediate crisis is over. If you are not sure about what to do, this section will help you decide whether veterinary help is needed and, if so, how urgently you should seek it. Potentially life threatening situations and conditions that might cause hidden pain are highlighted with easily recognizable symbols.

Part Three describes what to do in obvious emergencies. Emergencies are listed in alphabetical order, from **Aggression** through **Choking** and **Drowning** to **Poisoning** and, finally, **Vomiting**. For each emergency there is a description of how to give first aid and a chart to help you make the sometimes difficult decision about whether you should go to the vet as quickly as possible, whether you can wait until later in the day or until the next day, whether you should simply telephone your vet for advice, or can safely proceed solely with treatment at home.

Part Four describes how you can minimize risks to your dog, how to give medicines and how to prepare a first aid kit.

Acknowledgments

Veterinary medicine is a curious profession. A vet is expected to treat virtually any emergency that arises in any species of animal. This is one of the satisfactions and challenges of the work, and after practising veterinary medicine for a quarter of a century, I have seen my allotted share of emergencies.

At the same time, veterinary medicine is a highly specialized profession. Some vets concentrate on specific species – cats or horses for example. Others specialize in specific fields such as orthopedics, ophthalmology or dermatology. Emergency medicine and critical care is one of these specific fields.

When reading this book, you will come across some excellent advice and suggestions. When you do, more often than not they have probably come from Dr Suann Hosie of the Vancouver Animal Emergency Clinic in Vancouver, British Columbia, Canada. In both California and British Columbia, Dr Hosie has gained more experience in emergency medicine and critical care than virtually anyone else in Europe or North America. I asked Suann, a schoolmate from the Ontario Veterinary College, to read this book before I sent it to the publishers and she offered constructive advice on just about every single page. My appreciation is enormous.

PART ONE

THE ESSENTIALS OF FIRST AID

What is First Aid?

The objectives of first aid are to:

- Preserve life
- Prevent further injuries
- Control further potential damage
- Minimize pain and distress
- Promote recovery and repair
- Transport the dog safely to the veterinarian for professional care

Do not waste time trying to make an accurate diagnosis. Assess the situation quickly. Is the dog in further danger? Are you in danger if you try to help? Restrain the dog if necessary and remove it from the risk of further harm.

Assess the dog's condition. Look for obvious life threatening signs. When necessary, give emergency first aid on the spot. If someone else is available, they should get help by telephoning a vet and arranging to transport the injured dog.

An emergency is not the best time to ask your vet to make a house call. Whenever possible, it is almost always best to telephone the vet and take the injured dog to the nearest professionally equipped veterinary clinic.

What to Do First: The Basics of First Aid

When emergencies happen, carry out a quick physical examination of your dog. It is important to do so if you are to be accurate in your decision making and treating of emergencies. While your dog is fit and healthy, carry out these procedures:

- Restrain the dog
- Check breathing rate and rhythm
- Check heart rate or pulse
- Look for signs of shock

To make your practice examination as simple as possible, command your dog to **sit** or **stand** for each section of the examination. Do not try to do the entire examination in one session. Remember to reward your dog's obedience with a food snack, touch or praise. Give a reward after each step.

After you have carried out a brief but thorough emergency examination of the dog, you may need to administer first aid. The basics of first aid are:

- Artificial respiration
- Heart massage (cardiopulmonary resuscitation, or CPR)
- Cleaning wounds
- Applying bandages, splints, tourniquets and Elizabethan collars
- Lifting and transporting ill or injured dogs

In genuine emergencies, remember that your objectives are to save life, prevent further injury, pain or distress, and to help promote recovery.

RESTRAINT

Use as little restraint as necessary to carry out your examination. Too much restraint upsets many dogs and makes them uncooperative. Muzzle an injured dog if it looks frightened or has obviously painful injuries.

1. Approach the dog calmly. Talk to it reassuringly. Initially, avoid intimidating and potentially frightening direct eye contact.
2. While still talking, check the dog's expression to determine how frightened it is. Stroke the relaxed dog under the chin, then slip a leash around its neck. To examine a calm dog, hold it as shown in Figures 1 and 2. (If a dog leash is not available, use a tie or belt looped over the dog's neck.)

Fig. 1: Holding a large dog

Wrap your arm as far as possible around the dog's neck. This leaves your other hand free to examine the dog.

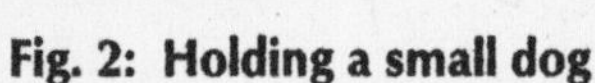

Fig. 2: Holding a small dog

Gently but firmly, grip the dog's muzzle. Apply a little pressure against the dog's body with the elbow of your free hand while you carry out your examination.

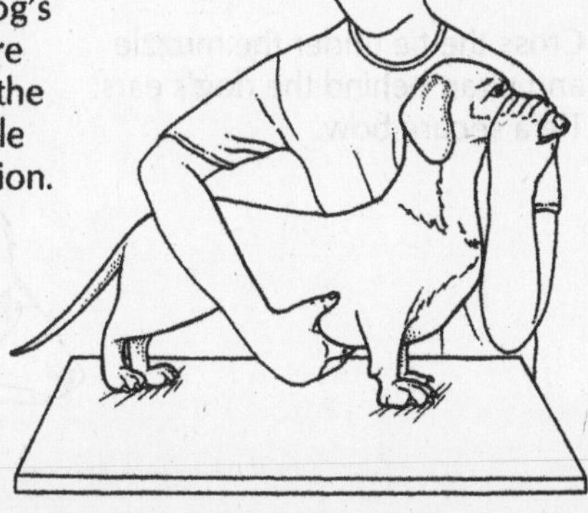

3. Muzzle the apprehensive dog by quickly looping a 50–75 cm (2–3 feet) length of soft, strong material over the dog's muzzle. (Use gauze bandage, a tie, torn cotton sheet or other soft material as a muzzle. Only in extreme emergencies use rope, twine or other harsh materials that may injure the dog's muzzle.)

Fig. 3: An emergency muzzle

Make a loop large enough to slip over the dog's muzzle.

Quickly slip this over the dog's muzzle and tighten. Do not tie a knot.

Cross the tie under the muzzle and wrap behind the dog's ears. Tie a secure bow.

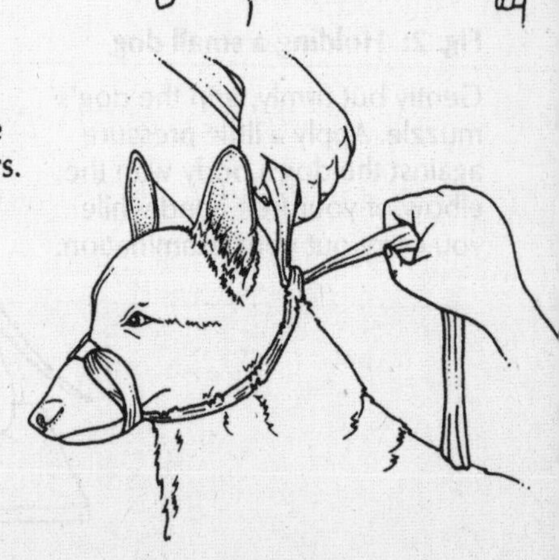

Fig. 4: Restraining a short muzzled or very small dog

Wrap a towel around the dog's neck. The towel can be pinned while you proceed with your examination.

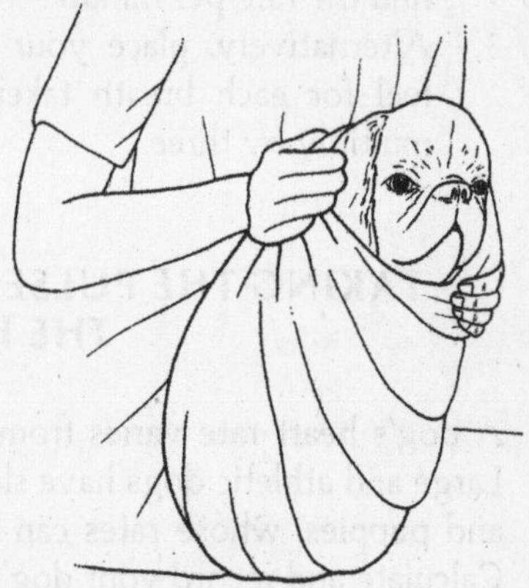

MONITORING BREATHING

Your dog normally breathes between ten and thirty times a minute. Small breeds and young dogs breathe more quickly than large or mature ones. The breathing rate increases dramatically after exercise or play. Calculate and record your dog's normal rate of breathing.

Dogs pant after exercise, when excited or worried, to eliminate excess heat, or when they are in pain. Panting is much more rapid than normal breathing. When calculating the normal breathing rate of your dog, monitor only regular breathing through the nose.

Dogs may appear to have difficulty breathing when they 'sneeze in reverse'. This curious behavior sounds like a severe asthma attack, but when it happens there is no cause for alarm.

1. While your dog is relaxed, watch how many times it breathes in twenty seconds. Only count breaths in or out, not both. Multiply by three to find the rate per minute.
2. If your dog has a fluffy coat or breathes so lightly that you cannot see any chest movement, hold a piece of tissue in front of its nose and count the number of times

the tissue moves in twenty seconds. Multiply by three to find the rate per minute.

3. Alternatively, place your hand on your dog's chest and feel for each breath taken in over twenty seconds and multiply by three.

TAKING THE PULSE AND MONITORING THE HEART

A dog's heart rate varies from sixty to 160 beats per minute. Large and athletic dogs have slower heart rates than small dogs and puppies, whose rates can be up to 200 beats per minute. Calculate and record your dog's normal resting heart rate.

The heart rate increases rapidly with excitement and exercise. It also increases when a dog is in pain, has a fever, is in the early stages of shock, has been poisoned, bitten, suffered an electric shock or has heart failure. Calculate your dog's resting heart rate when it is fit and healthy.

1. Speak reassuringly to the dog. Place your hand gently but firmly against its chest just behind its left elbow. Feel and count the heartbeats for twenty seconds. Multiply by three for the rate per minute.

Fig. 1: Large dog

Press firmly against the chest wall, especially in the case of overweight dogs or those with dense coats, moving your hand until you feel the heartbeat.

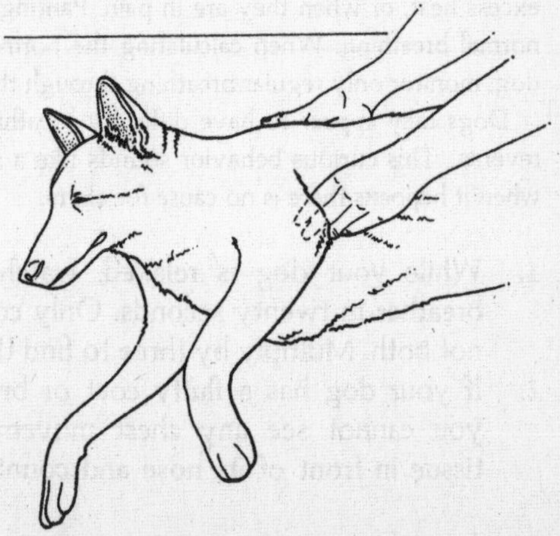

2. For smaller dogs, grasp the chest just behind the elbows. Feel for the heart. Count beats for twenty seconds and multiply by three for the rate per minute.

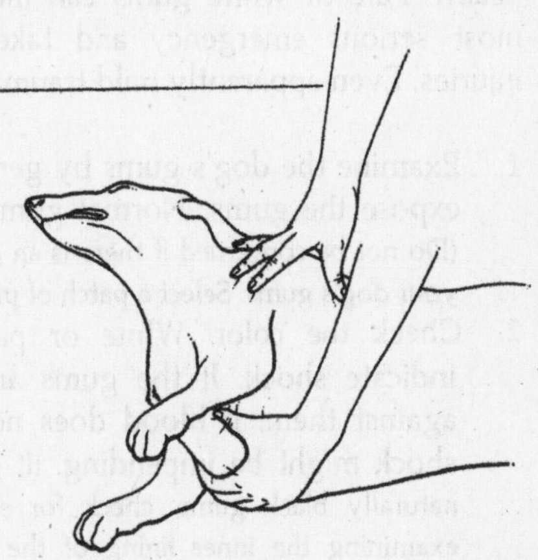

Fig. 2: Small dog

Gently squeeze the chest behind the elbows to feel for and then count the heart rate. The heartbeat is pronounced in lean breeds but more difficult to locate in fat dogs or those with thick skin or very dense coats.

3. Monitor the pulse by placing your fingers inside the hind leg where it joins the body. Move them around until you feel the pulse. Count for twenty seconds and multiply by three for the rate per minute.

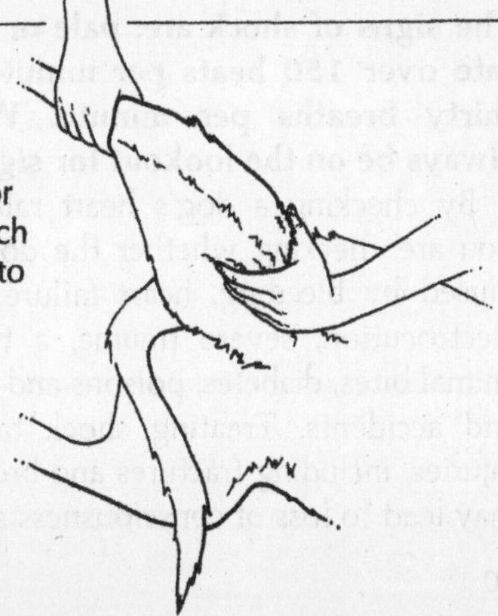

Fig. 3: Finding the pulse

Press your fingertips into the slight groove in the leg. Feel for the pulse. If you apply too much pressure, you will not be able to feel the pulse.

EXAMINING THE GUMS

The color of the gums is an important indicator of a dog's health. Pale or white gums can indicate shock. Shock is the most serious emergency and takes precedence over other injuries. Even apparently mild trauma can lead to shock.

1. Examine the dog's gums by gently lifting the upper lip to expose the gums. Normal gums are a healthy pink color. (Do not be concerned if there is an abundance of black pigment in your dog's gums. Select a patch of pink to examine.)
2. Check the color. White or pale gums almost certainly indicate shock. If the gums are pink, press your finger against them: if blood does not rush back immediately, shock might be impending. (If you have a Chow Chow with naturally black gums, check for shock by gently parting and examining the inner lining of the vagina, or by retracting the prepuce and examining the color of the penis.)

SHOCK

The signs of shock are: pale or white gums, a rapid heart rate over 150 beats per minute and fast breathing over thirty breaths per minute. Whatever the emergency, always be on the lookout for signs of shock.

By checking a dog's heart rate, breathing rate and gums you are checking whether the dog is in shock. Shock can be caused by bleeding, heart failure, vomiting and/or diarrhea, electrocution, severe trauma, a twisted stomach, insect and animal bites, diabetes, poisons and many other injuries, illnesses and accidents. Treating shock takes precedence over other injuries, including fractures and broken bones. Untreated shock may lead to loss of consciousness and death.

The signs of early shock are:

- Faster than normal breathing
- Faster than normal resting heart rate
- Pale or light pink gums
- Restlessness or anxiety
- Lethargy or weakness
- Slow capillary refill time – more than two seconds
- Normal or just subnormal rectal temperature

The signs of late shock are:

- Shallow, slow breathing
- Irregular heartbeat
- Very pale or blue gums
- Lack of response
- Extreme weakness or unconsciousness
- Very slow capillary refill – more than four seconds
- Very cool body temperature – less than 36.7°C/98°F

Slow down the potentially catastrophic effects of shock by doing the following:

1. Place the dog on its side with head extended.
2. Elevate the hindquarters using pillows or towels.
3. Stop any obvious bleeding by applying pressure with an absorbent pad, or by applying a tourniquet if necessary. (See page 27.)
4. Give artificial respiration or heart massage if necessary. (See page 14.)
5. Prevent loss of body heat by wrapping the dog in a warm blanket.
6. Transport to the nearest veterinarian immediately. If the dog is in deep shock; keep it cradled with limbs elevated above the heart.

- **Do not give anything to eat or drink**
- **Do not let a conscious dog wander about**

ANAPHYLACTIC SHOCK

Anaphylactic shock may be brought on by insect stings, drugs, or, very rarely, by food.

Recognizing anaphylactic shock:

- Has the dog just had an injection or been given medicines?
- Has it possibly been stung by an insect?
- Has it just eaten and is having difficulty breathing?
- Is the dog retching or vomiting?
- Does it have sudden diarrhea?
- Is the dog collapsing?
- Are the gums blue?
- Is the dog showing signs of shock?

1. Keep the airway open.
2. Give artificial respiration and heart massage if necessary. (See page 14.)
3. If the dog's lungs fill with liquid, it will start making gurgling sounds while trying to breathe. Suspend the dog for ten seconds by its hind legs to try to clear the airway.
4. Get immediate veterinary assistance. (Urgent treatment is essential. The veterinarian will give drugs to stop the allergic swelling in the air passages.)

A less urgent allergic reaction to bites and injections causes the face to swell and become itchy. Sometimes the site of the bite or injection is itchy or hot and painful. Prevent your dog from mutilating itself by using an Elizabethan collar (see page 29) and monitor its reaction. Allergic reactions can suddenly develop into life threatening anaphylactic shock.

WHEN TO GIVE ARTIFICIAL RESPIRATION AND HEART MASSAGE

If a dog's brain does not receive oxygen for several minutes because either the heart or breathing has stopped, permanent brain damage results. This is one of the very few circumstances when the immediate provision of first aid may be life saving. Artificial respiration given together with heart massage is called cardiopulmonary resuscitation, or CPR. The abbreviation CPR is used throughout this book.

Assess the situation
Causes of unconsciousness that may require CPR include: **Choking, Electrocution, Near-drowning, Congestive heart failure, Smoke inhalation, Poisoning, Blood loss, Concussion, Fainting, Shock** and **Diabetes.**
(Strokes and heart attacks, the most common reasons for giving artificial respiration and heart massage to humans, are both uncommon in dogs.)

Assess the dog's consciousness:

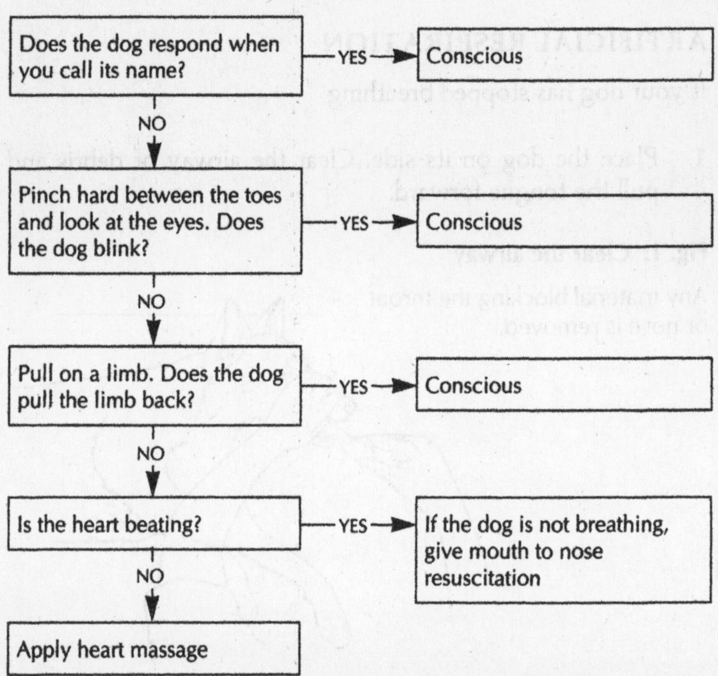
Does the dog respond when you call its name?
YES
Conscious
NO
Pinch hard between the toes and look at the eyes. Does the dog blink?
YES
Conscious
NO
Pull on a limb. Does the dog pull the limb back?
YES
Conscious
NO
Is the heart beating?
YES
If the dog is not breathing, give mouth to nose resuscitation
NO
Apply heart massage

HOW TO GIVE CARDIOPULMONARY RESUSCITATION (CPR)

Artificial respiration (mouth to nose) and heart massage are two life saving procedures often called cardiopulmonary resuscitation or CPR. If your dog is not breathing and has no heartbeat, give CPR. To be effective, heart massage must be administered rhythmically with mouth to nose respiration.

Do not attempt either procedure unless it is obvious that the dog is unconscious and will die without your help.

(Even when the best medical equipment is available it can be difficult to restart a dog's heart and breathing. If there has been massive internal bleeding, for example, it is virtually impossible. If you are unsuccessful, do not think it has been your fault.)

ARTIFICIAL RESPIRATION

If your dog has stopped breathing:

1. Place the dog on its side. Clear the airway of debris and pull the tongue forward.

Fig. 1: Clear the airway

Any material blocking the throat or nose is removed.

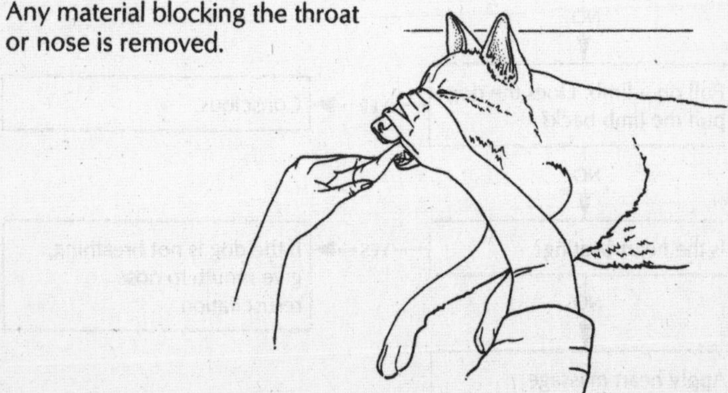

2. Close the dog's mouth. With your hand around the muzzle place your mouth over the dog's nose and blow in until you see the chest expand.

Fig. 2: Breathe into the dog's lungs

Your hand on the muzzle creates an airtight seal.

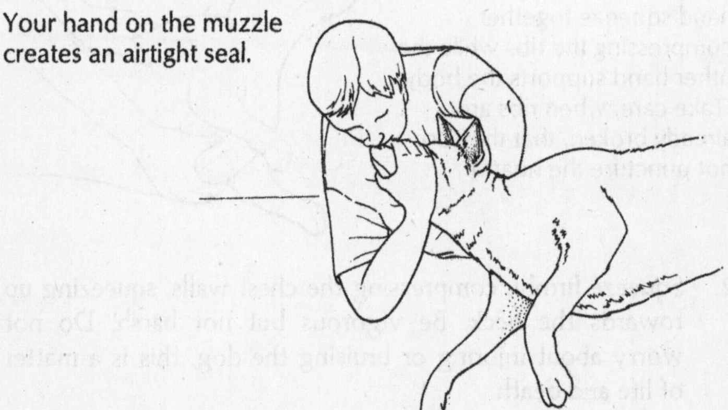

3. Take your mouth away and let the lungs deflate.
4. Repeat this procedure ten to twenty times per minute.
5. Check the pulse every ten seconds to ensure the heart is still beating.
6. If the heart is not beating, give heart massage in conjunction with artificial respiration.
7. Get professional veterinary attention as soon as possible.

HEART MASSAGE

Feel for a heartbeat or pulse. Squeeze the gums and see if the squeezed area refills with blood when you remove your finger. If the dog's heart has stopped:

Small dogs

1. Place the dog on its side with the head lower than the body if possible. Grasp the chest between your thumb and

fingers just behind the elbows. Place your other hand on the dog's back.

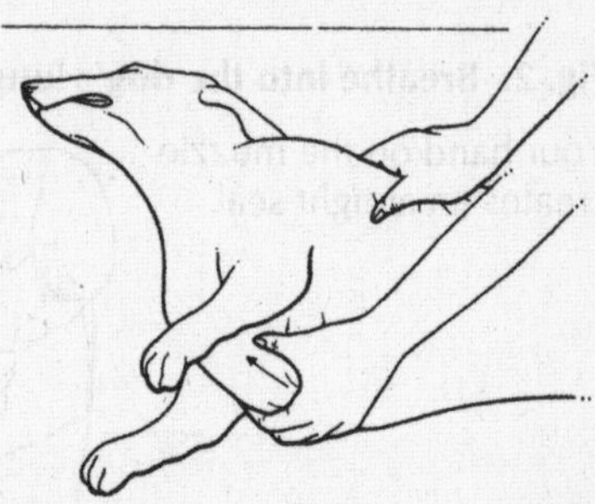

Fig. 1: Heart massage

The thumb and fingers of one hand squeeze together, compressing the ribs while the other hand supports the body. (Take care, when ribs are already broken, that they do not puncture the heart.)

2. Squeeze firmly, compressing the chest walls, squeezing up towards the neck. Be vigorous but not harsh. Do not worry about injuring or bruising the dog, this is a matter of life and death.
3. Repeat this pumping action 120 times a minute using quick, firm pumps.
4. Apply heart massage for fifteen seconds, then mouth to nose respiration for ten seconds.
5. Check for a pulse. Continue heart massage until the pulse returns, then concentrate wholly on artificial respiration.
6. Get veterinary attention as soon as possible.

Medium sized and large, deep chested dogs

1. Place the dog on its side with the head lower than the body if possible. Place the heel of one hand on the chest just behind the elbow. Place the heel of your other hand on top of the first hand.

Fig. 2: Hands in position

Pressure is applied briskly and firmly, pushing both down to massage the heart and forward to push blood towards the brain.

2. Press firmly, compressing the chest walls, pushing blood up towards the neck. Be vigorous but not harsh. Do not worry about injuring or bruising the dog, this is a matter of life and death.
3. Repeat this pumping action a hundred times a minute using quick, firm pumps.
4. Apply heart massage for fifteen seconds then mouth to nose respiration for ten seconds.
5. Check for a pulse. Continue heart massage until the pulse returns, then concentrate wholly on artificial respiration.
6. Get veterinary attention as soon as possible.

Large, flat chested or very fat dogs

1. Place the dog on its back with the head lower than the body if possible. Put the heel of one hand on the breastbone. Place the heel of your other hand on top of the first hand.
2. Press firmly, both down and towards the head, pushing blood to the brain. Be vigorous. On large dogs this requires strength. Unless there are rib or chest injuries, do not worry about injuring or bruising the dog.

Fig. 3: Firm force

Use the strength of your body to compress the chest. In very large or obese dogs you may have to press so hard you risk breaking a rib. This is an acceptable risk in a life and death situation.

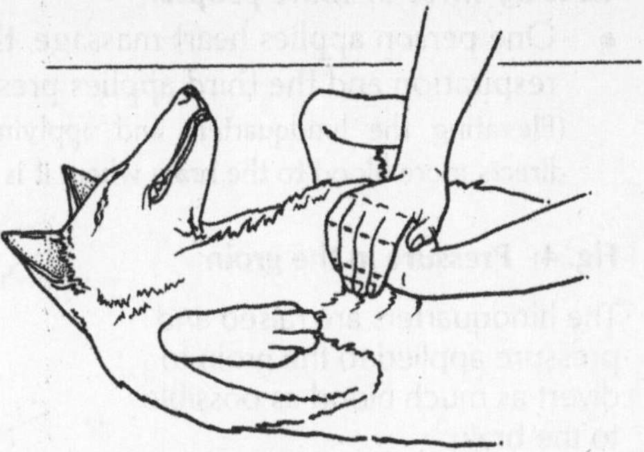

3. Repeat this pumping action eighty times a minute using quick, firm pumps. Hold each pump for a count of two

and release for a count of one. If you are pumping efficiently you will feel physically exhausted within minutes.

4. Apply heart massage for fifteen seconds then mouth to nose respiration for ten seconds.
5. Check for a pulse. Continue heart massage until the pulse returns, then concentrate wholly on artificial respiration.
6. Get veterinary attention as soon as possible.

CPR by one person:

- Massage the heart for fifteen seconds
- Give mouth to nose respiration for ten seconds
- Continue until the heartbeat and breathing resumes
- Keep the dog warm and get veterinary help immediately

CPR by two people:

- One person applies heart massage for five seconds then stops
- The second person gives one breath into the dog's nose
- Continue these procedures rhythmically
- When the heart starts, continue artificial respiration
- The heart massager arranges transportation to the veterinarian while artificial respiration continues

CPR by three or more people:

- One person applies heart massage, the second artificial respiration and the third applies pressure in the groin.
  (Elevating the hindquarters and applying pressure to the groin directs more blood to the brain where it is needed most.)

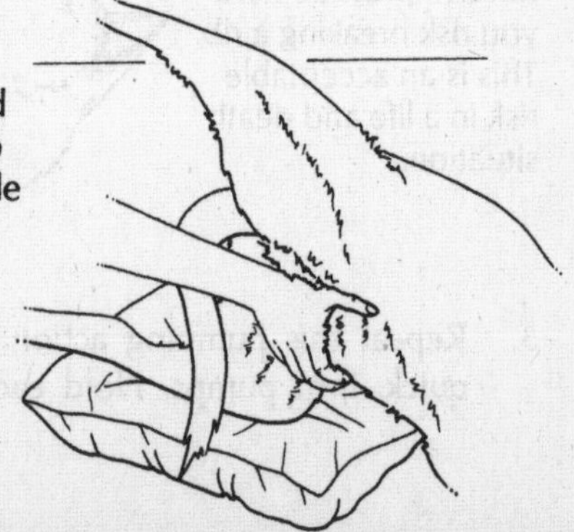

Fig. 4: Pressure in the groin

The hindquarters are raised and pressure applied to the groin to divert as much blood as possible to the brain.

HOW TO CLEAN WOUNDS

When examining your dog you may come across an injury that needs your attention. Injuries are often painful. Take care to cause as little discomfort as possible, as even the most docile dog may bite when frightened or in pain. Practice first aid when your dog is fit and healthy by examining for wounds and then cleaning a designated area as you would if there were a genuine injury.

The two most common types of wounds are **closed**, where the skin is not broken, and **open**, where the skin is broken. **Fractures** can accompany either type of injury. With most wounds there is the danger of infection.

CLOSED WOUNDS

Closed wounds can be deceptive. Because the skin is not broken it looks like there is little damage. Do not underestimate a closed wound, it may look insignificant but underneath there can be dramatic internal injuries, the full extent of which may not be apparent for days. Even when wounds look minor, telephone your veterinarian and get professional advice.

The signs of closed wounds are:

- Swelling
- Pain
- Discoloration caused by bruising under the skin
- Increased heat in a specific location
- Superficial damage such as scratches to the skin

First aid for closed wounds:

1. Apply a cool compress to the wound as soon as possible after the injury. (A bag of frozen peas makes an ideal compress because it thaws faster than ice and molds to the contour of the injured area.)
2. If there is superficial skin damage such as scratching, clean

with salt water (1 teaspoon salt to half a pint of water) or 3% hydrogen peroxide. A non-stinging antiseptic liquid or spray may be applied after cleaning.
3. Look for other hidden injuries, especially if your dog has been hit by a car. Contact your veterinarian for further advice.

Fig. 1: Apply an ice pack

Using a bag of frozen vegetables, a towel soaked in cold water or ice wrapped in a towel, apply the cool compress to the injured area.

OPEN WOUNDS

When the skin has been broken, underlying tissue is exposed to dirt and bacteria. There is a great risk that these wounds will become infected. Give immediate first aid to stop bleeding, minimize further damage and control pain, then see your veterinarian as soon as possible. Remember, although open wounds may appear more serious, internal damage under closed wounds can be equally life threatening.

The signs of open wounds are:

- Broken skin, sometimes only a puncture
- Pain
- Bleeding
- Increased licking or attention to a specific area

First aid for open wounds:

Wounds bleeding severely

1. Stop the bleeding by applying pressure. If first aid material is available use a non-stick pad, otherwise use any clean, absorbing material such as kitchen towel or a tea cloth. Do not remove the blood-soaked absorbing material. This disturbs the clot that has formed and bleeding may recur. Do not use disinfectants or antiseptics.

Fig. 1: Apply direct pressure to the bleeding wound

Press an absorbent pad held in your hand directly on the wound for two minutes. This allows a clot to form.

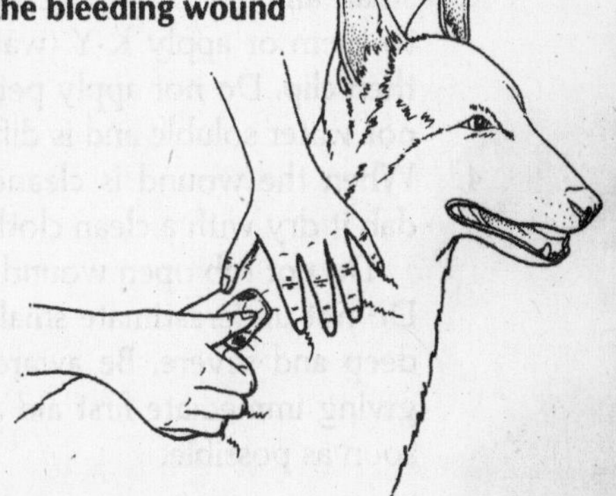

2. Add more absorbing padding if necessary and when possible elevate the injury above the dog's heart. **Do not elevate a leg if there is a possible fracture.**
3. Treat for shock (see page 10).

Detailed instructions on how to control bleeding on different parts of the body, how to find pressure points and how to apply a tourniquet are given under the heading **Bleeding** on page 76.

Wounds not bleeding severely

1. Flush minor wounds with 3% hydrogen peroxide, salt water, antiseptic or clean bottled or tap water.
2. Remove obvious dirt, gravel, splinters or other material

from the wound, using tweezers or clean fingers. Clean the skin and hair around the wound with soap and water. Do not pull large objects like arrows or pieces of wood or metal out of open wounds – uncontrollable bleeding could follow. Go directly to the nearest veterinarian. (A water pik is ideal for cleaning wounds. Alternatively, use a clean-hand-held garden spray water bottle with the nozzle turned to 'jet' rather than 'mist'.)

3. If hair is getting in the wound, cut it when it is damp for easy removal. Alternatively, lubricate the scissors with a small amount of petroleum jelly so that cut hair adheres to them or apply K-Y (water soluble) jelly to the wound, then clip. Do not apply petroleum jelly to the wound. It is not water soluble and is difficult to remove later.
4. When the wound is cleaned and superficially disinfected, dab it dry with a clean cloth.

   Do not rub open wounds, you may cause more damage. Do not underestimate small open wounds, injuries may be deep and severe. Be aware of the risk of infection. After giving immediate first aid always see your veterinarian as soon as possible.

For more details on how to treat specific wounds see **Fish-hooks** on page 121, **Puncture wounds** on page 156 and **Bones** on page 83.

HOW TO APPLY BANDAGES

Bandages keep wounds dry and protect them from further injuries, including self-inflicted damage caused by biting, chewing and excessive licking. They also prevent injuries from becoming more contaminated and absorb seeping fluids. Bandaging provides constant mild pressure to control pain or bleeding and prevents pockets of serum building up under the skin. A bandage consists of three layers; an absorbent pad, gauze and adhesive tape.

Absorbent pad

Sterile, non-stick pads are best but in emergencies use any clean, dirt-free absorbent material as a pad. Face cloths and cotton towels are good absorbers, paper products are not so good and are difficult to remove later from the wound. If only paper products are available, such as facial or toilet tissue or paper towels, apply K-Y (water soluble) jelly to the wound before applying the pad. Use antiseptic cream, lotion or spray only on minor wounds.

Gauze

Gauze, wrapped not too tightly around the absorbent pad, secures the pad to the injury. Most types of good gauze stretch. Do not stretch gauze tightly when wrapping an injury, as this cuts off circulation to the area.

Adhesive tape

Adhesive tape secures the gauze wrapping and absorbent pad to the injured part of the dog's body. It should be secure enough that the dog cannot chew it off but not so tight that it cuts the circulation of blood to the region. Many adhesive tapes are elastic. Take extra care when using elastic adhesive bandage, as wounds often swell. A well applied bandage might be cutting off circulation a few hours later.

GENERAL BANDAGE TECHNIQUE

1. After cleaning, disinfecting and drying the wound, place the absorbent pad over the affected area.

Fig. 1: Apply an absorbent pad

The wound has been cleaned and the pad generously covers the entire injured area.

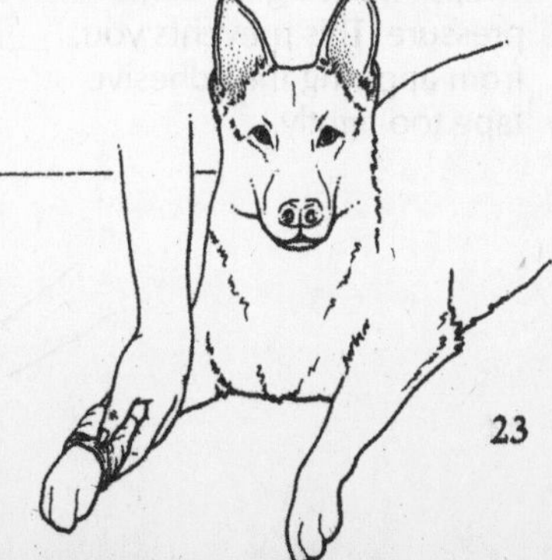

2. Starting over one edge of the pad, wrap gauze around so that the pad does not slip from its designated area.

Fig. 2: Wrap gauze over the pad

The first wrap secures the pad. Each wrap covers about one third of the previous wrap. Continue until the entire pad is covered, together with undamaged tissue on either side.

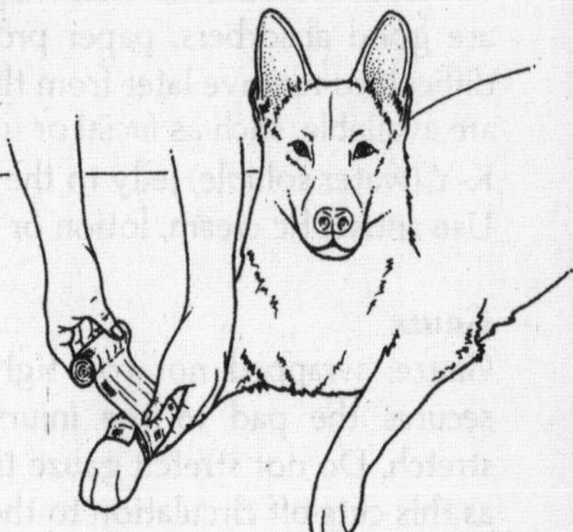

3. Hold the end of the gauze with one hand to prevent it unravelling and apply the first wrap of adhesive tape at that point. Continue wrapping but extend the adhesive tape beyond the gauze at both ends of the bandage, catching bits of hair at these places. This helps to secure the bandage and prevents it from shifting.

Fig. 3: Secure the bandage with adhesive tape

Place two fingers under the bandage as you wrap, then remove them and continue wrapping, using the same pressure. This prevents you from applying the adhesive tape too tightly.

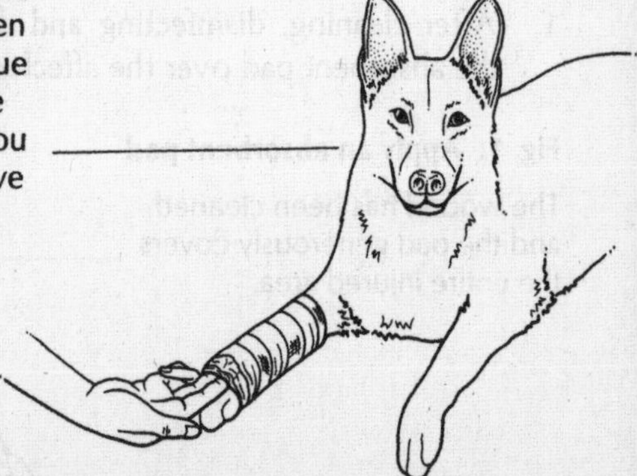

4. Keep the bandage clean and dry. Cover it with a plastic bag when your dog goes outside. Do not let a bandage get wet. Do not use elastic bands to keep the plastic bag on. If left on they cut off circulation and cause grave injuries.
5. Unless your veterinarian tells you otherwise, change bandages daily. Do not leave a bandage on for any excessive period of time. To do so increases the risk of infection or tissue death from poor circulation.
6. Bandaged wounds are highly susceptible to infection. If a wound becomes swollen or discharges pus, go to your vet. Remove bandages and get immediate veterinary attention if there is an unpleasant smell coming from the wound.
7. Keep your dog quiet and restrict its exercise until healing has been completed and the bandage removed. Do not let your dog exercise freely while a wound is bandaged.
8. If your dog chews its bandage your veterinarian can provide a plastic Elizabethan collar to be worn until the bandage is removed. Do not let your dog chew at a bandage.

See page 29 for how to make an Elizabethan collar.

HOW TO MAKE A SPLINT

A temporary splint reduces further damage while you transport your dog to the veterinary clinic. It should be solid enough to hold the leg in position but not so tight that it cuts off circulation. Do not try to set or reposition a broken bone with a splint, this would be extremely painful for the dog. Your veterinarian will do so using potent pain killers or an anesthetic. Practice putting a splint on your dog only if it has an amenable character and is willing to let you do so.

1. Your objective is to immobilize the broken bone. Use any splint material available; magazines, newspapers, rolled cardboard, garden sticks, even cutlery if necessary. The best splint is made by thickly wrapping large quantities of cotton wool around the fracture site.

Using magazines and newspapers:

2. Roll the splinting material around the entire leg and fasten the roll with tape. Attempt to cover the joints above and below the suspected fracture site. Make sure the splint is tight enough that it does not slip off when the dog is moved. Do not tape so tightly that circulation is cut off.

Fig. 1: Stabilize the fracture

The splint material immobilizes the fracture. It does not set it.

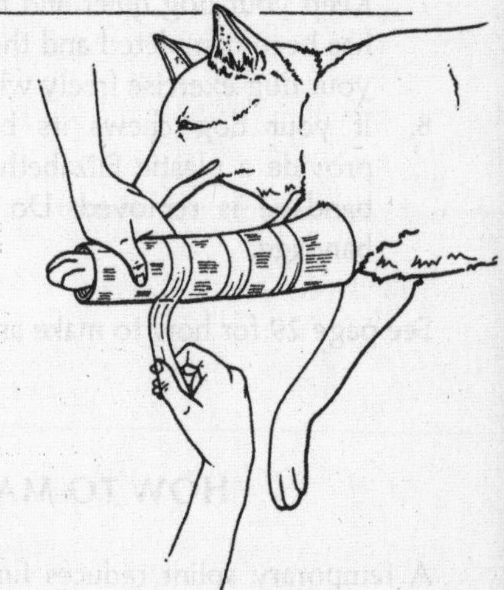

Using towels, sheets or cotton wool:

3. Fold the sheet or towel to give it thickness and slide it under the injured leg. Wrap the material around the leg and tape it in place. Repeat with another piece of material until the surrounding thickness immobilizes the leg. (Take care that you move the leg as little as possible.)

Fig. 2: A fabric splint

Safety pins or strips of torn fabric can be used to hold the splinting fabric together when tape is not available.

If you suspect a fracture, try to immobilize the affected area with a splint before transporting your dog to the veterinarian.

If bone is visible, apply a clean pad over it before splinting. Do not put any ointment on this pad.

After any traumatic injury, always look for shock. Shock is life threatening. Treating shock takes precedence over splinting bones.

HOW TO APPLY A TOURNIQUET

Tourniquets are dangerous and can do more harm than good. Whenever possible, use pressure to stop bleeding. For suspected poisonous snake bites, use ice packs and immobilization rather than a tourniquet to control the spread of poison around the body. Apply a tourniquet only when bleeding from a leg is devastating and you cannot stop it by any other means. Do not practice applying a tourniquet to your dog, it could be painful and unpleasant.

1. Wrap a piece of fabric (a tie, soft belt, torn sheet or gauze) above the bleeding wound and tie a knot.

Fig. 1: Tie a tight knot

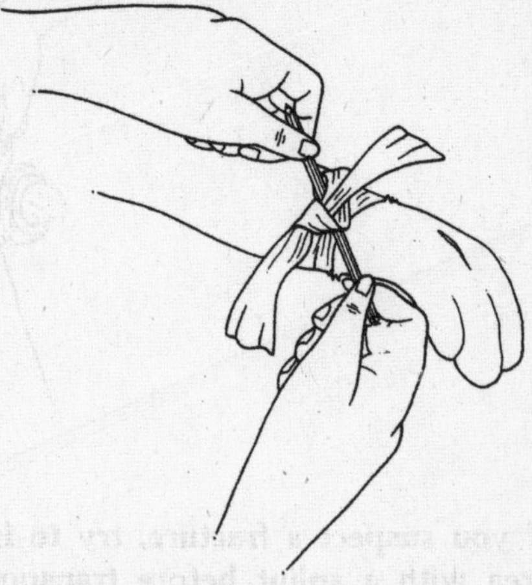

2. Slip a pen, pencil, stick, or other firm and slender material into the wrapped material and twist it until the bleeding stops.
3. Tie down the pencil with another piece of material, keeping the bandage firm and tight. Get immediate veterinary help.

Fig. 2: The tourniquet is tied in place

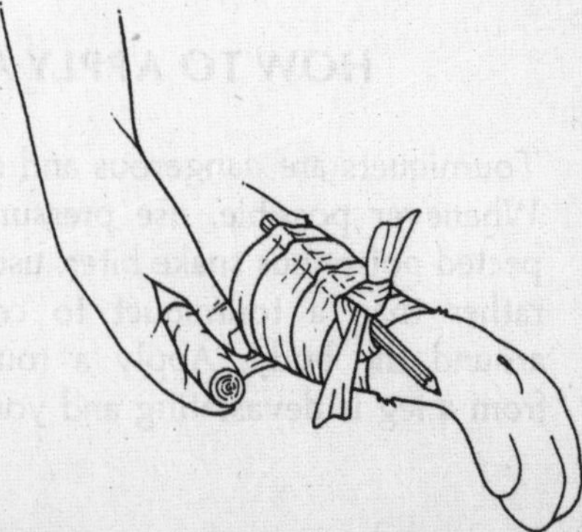

A tight tourniquet cuts off the blood supply. If it is left on too long it could lead to the 'death' of the limb.

HOW TO MAKE AN ELIZABETHAN COLLAR

Occasionally, it will be necessary for you to prevent your dog from licking or chewing itself, or pawing at and rubbing its face after an injury and before you can get to your veterinarian. Emergency Elizabethan collars can be made by cutting the bottom out of an appropriately sized plastic plant pot or by rolling up a fan-shaped piece of hard cardboard. The Elizabethan collar is secured by tape to the dog's collar.

1. Cut out the bottom of a plastic plant pot. Make four holes in the pot and slip pieces of gauze through them. Make sure the cut edges are not jagged and will not injure the dog's neck. Line the cut edges with adhesive tape.
2. Alternatively, cut a piece of cardboard in a fan shape then roll it up and tape or tie it together in a cone.

Fig. 1: Preparing an Elizabethan collar from a plant pot.

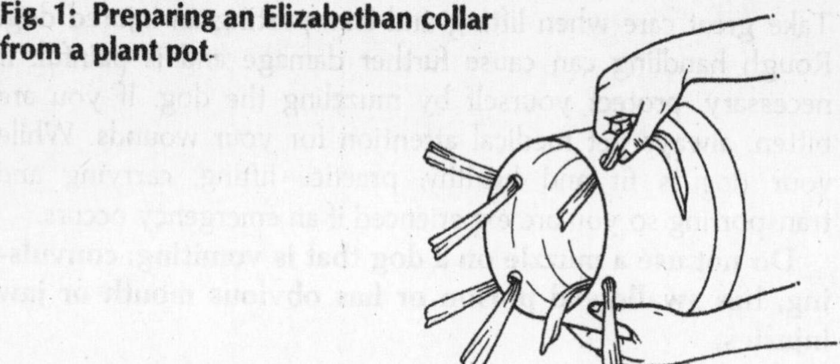

3. Make sure the dog is wearing a collar. If not, create a makeshift collar with a piece of gauze tied loosely around the neck. Slip the flower pot over the dog's head and tie it with the four tapes to the dog's collar.

Fig. 2: Secure the Elizabethan collar to the dog

Make sure it is not too tight. The collar should be large enough to fit just over the dog's head.

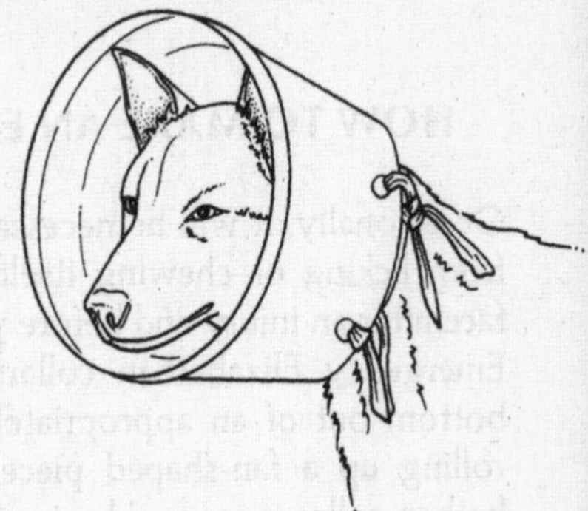

4. Keep the Elizabethan collar on the dog until you see your veterinarian.

HOW TO LIFT, CARRY AND TRANSPORT A DOG

Take great care when lifting and transporting an injured dog. Rough handling can cause further damage and is painful. If necessary, protect yourself by muzzling the dog. If you are bitten, always get medical attention for your wounds. While your dog is fit and healthy, practice lifting, carrying and transporting so you are experienced if an emergency occurs.

Do not use a muzzle on a dog that is vomiting, convulsing, has swallowed poison or has obvious mouth or jaw injuries.

MINOR INJURIES

Small dogs:

1. If an injured dog is willing to walk to the car, let it do so.
2. Lift a small dog by holding its collar or neck with one

hand while using your other hand to support the back and body.

3. Cradle the dog against your body and with your hand under the chest lift it up.

Fig. 1: Lifting a small dog

One hand controls and supports the neck, preventing the dog from turning and biting. The other supports the chest and abdomen. Pressing against your body protects the dog's back.

Medium dogs:

1. Place one arm around the dog's neck and draw it towards you.
2. Place your other arm under the dog's groin and draw its body towards you.
3. With your own back as straight as possible, prevent the dog from wriggling with your arms. Lift the dog by standing straight up. This protects your back.

Fig. 2: Lifting a medium sized dog

The arm around the neck controls head movement while the arm under the abdomen supports and controls the hindquarters. The dog is pressed firmly against the first aider's body.

Large dogs:

1. Slip one arm under the dog's neck around to the leg on the far side. Make sure you do not interfere with breathing.
2. Slip your other arm under the dog's rump, firmly grasping the far leg.
3. Press your arms towards each other and draw the dog close to you. With your back straight, stand up using your leg muscles to support the dog's weight.

Fig. 3: Lifting a large dog

Avoid pressure on the chest or abdomen. One hand wraps around to the shoulder muscles while the other wraps around the hind leg muscles. These bear the dog's weight when it is lifted.

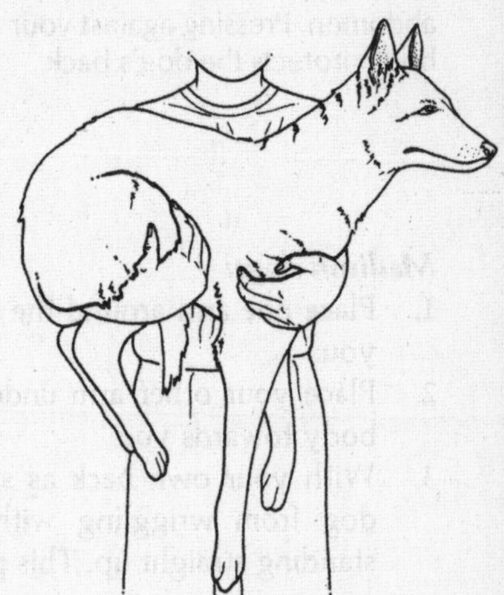

CRITICAL INJURIES

Critical injuries include all those that prevent the dog from moving itself and obvious serious injuries such as fractures or paralysis. Take extreme care when lifting a dog with potentially serious physical injuries:

- Support the back
- Keep broken legs up
- Keep injured chests down with the best lung up. (If the chest is injured and legs broken, the injured chest takes priority)
- Let the dog find its own comfortable breathing position

1. Keep the injured dog's back towards you.
2. Slide the dog on to a board. (An ironing board is useful for large dogs, but make sure the board fits in your car.)

Fig. 4: A makeshift stretcher

Slip one hand under the dog's chest and the other under its rump. Gently pull it on to the stretcher.

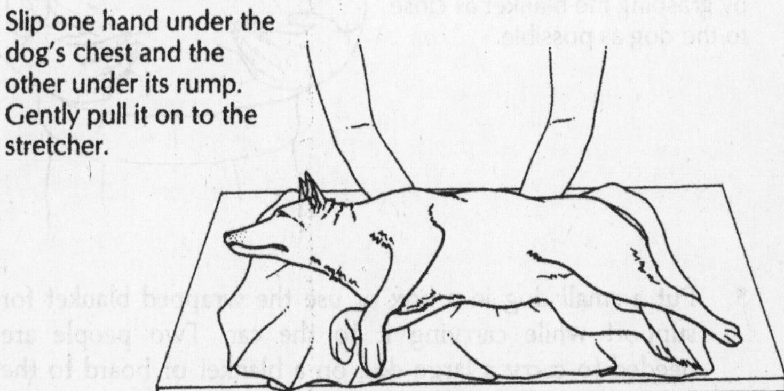

3. If additional help is not available, tie the dog to the stretcher. (Removable shelving makes a useful stretcher.)

Fig. 5: Secure the dog to the stretcher

Place ropes or strips of cloth under the stretcher before sliding the dog on, then tie the dog to the board. Do not tie its neck down.

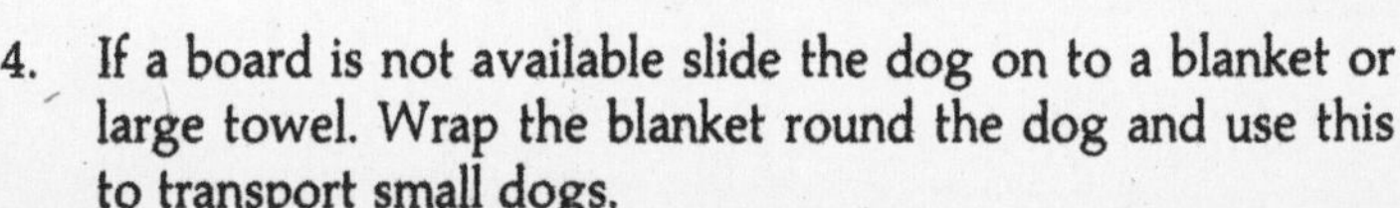

4. If a board is not available slide the dog on to a blanket or large towel. Wrap the blanket round the dog and use this to transport small dogs.

Fig. 6: A blanket stretcher

Supporting both the front and rear of the body, the small dog is lifted and pulled on to the folded blanket. The dog is lifted by grasping the blanket as close to the dog as possible.

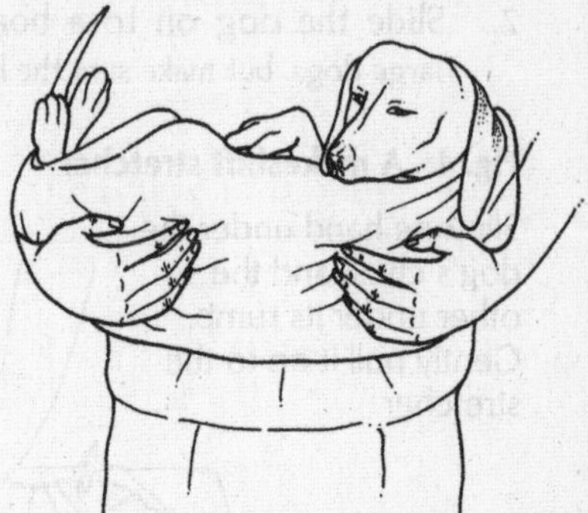

5. Put a small dog in a box or use the wrapped blanket for support while carrying it to the car. Two people are needed to carry a large dog on a blanket or board to the car. Rest the dog with its back against the car seat.
6. Restrain the dog during transportation. If someone is not available to sit with the injured dog, pack pillows and blankets around it. Cover the dog with a blanket to conserve heat and reduce the risk of shock. (In cold weather turn on your car heater to keep the dog warm.)

- **If injuries are serious, do not waste time looking for items of support.**
- **Get to the veterinary clinic as quickly as possible but avoid sudden movements that may cause further injuries.**
- **When lifting and transporting an injured dog, avoid bending or twisting its body.**

PART TWO

WHAT TO DO NEXT

Deciding If and When Your Dog Needs Veterinary Attention

Deciding whether your dog needs veterinary attention and, if so, when, can be difficult. For each emergency in this book there is a decision chart to help you decide what to do after you have provided first aid.

If your dog's life is in danger, if there is a risk of permanent injury or if your dog's problem causes obvious or hidden pain, the decision chart instructs you:

See a vet NOW 
NOW

This means as soon as possible. Telephone ahead to make sure a veterinarian is available and get the dog to the clinic as soon as safety allows.

Other problems, although not as urgent, still require immediate veterinary treatment. For these conditions the decision chart indicates:

See a vet same day 
12

For some conditions an appointment can wait until the next morning, but still make that telephone call as soon as possible.

There are other emergencies that need less urgent, follow-up veterinary treatment. The decision chart indicates:

See a vet within 24 hours 

In these circumstances an appointment can wait until the next day.

Many conditions are neither life threatening nor cause pain, but with veterinary treatment the dog's life can be made more comfortable or prolonged. In these situations the decision chart indicates:

See a vet soon 

The appointment can wait until a time convenient for both you and your veterinarian.

Many emergencies can be handled at home without the need for professional treatment. Although the chances of complications arising are small, hidden problems are possible and these may vary depending on where you live, the season of the year, and the age, size, sex or even breed of your dog. In these circumstances the decision chart indicates:

Phone for advice 

Some incidents can be diagnosed and treated at home. Follow the instructions carefully. If your dog is not improving rapidly, even with your good care, contact your veterinarian.

Further Examination

WHEN, WHY AND HOW TO CARRY OUT A HEAD-TO-TAIL EXAMINATION

Once you have given life saving first aid, or after you have examined the dog and found its life not to be in imminent danger, it is important to carry out a further examination, looking for less obvious but potentially serious, painful or distressing conditions. While your dog is fit and healthy carry out the following procedures:

- Observe behavior and responses
- Listen to sounds
- Watch activities and movement
- Smell odors
- Take the temperature
- Examine the eyes, ears, nose and mouth
- Examine the head and neck
- Examine the body and limbs
- Examine the tail and anus
- Examine the skin and coat
- Observe gastrointestinal changes
- Monitor toilet habits
- Monitor eating and drinking changes
- Observe weight changes

Make your practice examination as simple as possible. Don't try to do everything in one session, your dog will get bored and try to leave. Remember to reward your dog's obedience with food treats, words of praise and petting. Give a reward after each step.

In real emergencies you will often not have time to carry out a complete head-to-tail examination, but by knowing what to do you can choose which parts are most important to carry out.

HOW TO TAKE A DOG'S TEMPERATURE

A dog's normal temperature is between 38.1 and 39.2°C/ 100.5 and 102.5°F. Nervousness and exercise raise body temperature, as do excess heat and infections. Temperatures below normal are caused by exposure to cold weather but also by shock. Record your dog's normal resting temperature. (When possible use a digital thermometer. They are accurate and easy to read.)

1. If using a glass thermometer, shake it down, lubricate the tip with K-Y (water soluble) jelly and, using a slight rotating action, insert the thermometer about 2.5 cm (1 inch) into the dog's rectum.
2. Keep hold of the thermometer and the dog's tail, wait for ninety seconds then remove, wipe clean and read. Disinfect the thermometer after each use.

- **Do not try to take a dog's temperature by mouth.**
- **Do not take the dog's temperature if it deeply resents your attempt to do so.**

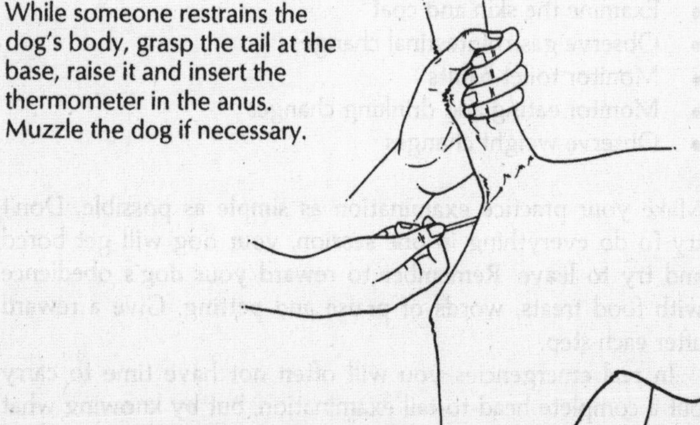

Fig. 1:

While someone restrains the dog's body, grasp the tail at the base, raise it and insert the thermometer in the anus. Muzzle the dog if necessary.

TEMPERATURE RANGE

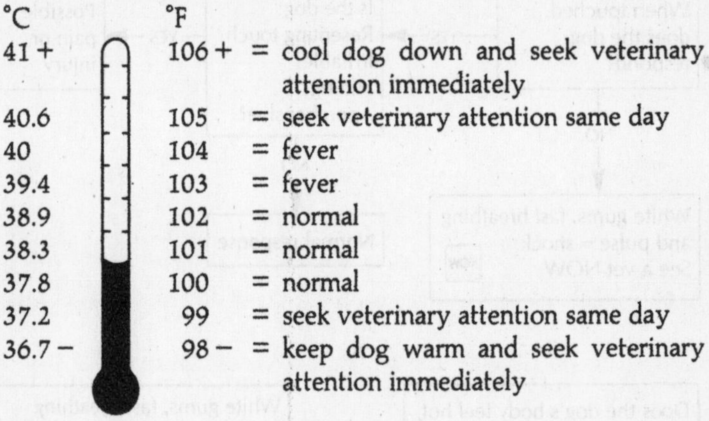

°C	°F		
41 +	106 +	=	cool dog down and seek veterinary attention immediately
40.6	105	=	seek veterinary attention same day
40	104	=	fever
39.4	103	=	fever
38.9	102	=	normal
38.3	101	=	normal
37.8	100	=	normal
37.2	99	=	seek veterinary attention same day
36.7 –	98 –	=	keep dog warm and seek veterinary attention immediately

BEHAVIOR AND RESPONSE

Any change from normal behavior is cause for concern, even attractive changes. If your dog is normally aloof but now wants to be with you, assume that it has been frightened or feels unwell.

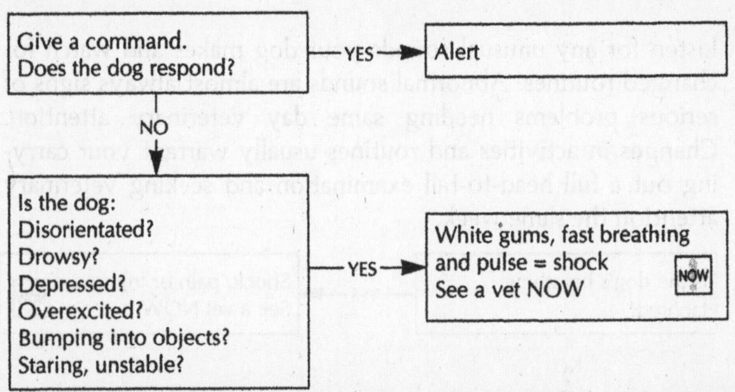
Give a command.
Does the dog respond?
YES
Alert
NO
Is the dog:
Disorientated?
Drowsy?
Depressed?
Overexcited?
Bumping into objects?
Staring, unstable?
YES
White gums, fast breathing
and pulse = shock
See a vet NOW
NOW

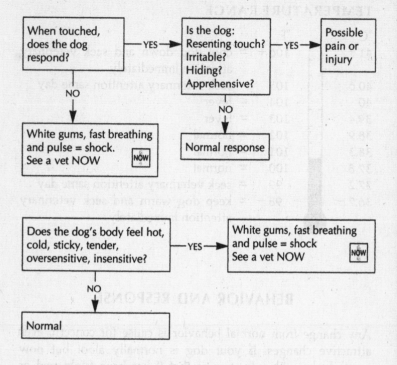

When touched, does the dog respond?
- YES → Is the dog: Resenting touch? Irritable? Hiding? Apprehensive?
  - YES → Possible pain or injury
  - NO → Normal response
- NO → White gums, fast breathing and pulse = shock. See a vet NOW (NOW)

Does the dog's body feel hot, cold, sticky, tender, oversensitive, insensitive?
- YES → White gums, fast breathing and pulse = shock See a vet NOW (NOW)
- NO → Normal

SOUNDS AND ACTIVITIES

Listen for any unusual sounds your dog makes and watch for changed routines. Abnormal sounds are almost always signs of serious problems needing same day veterinary attention. Changes in activities and routines usually warrant your carrying out a full head-to-tail examination and seeking veterinary attention the same week.

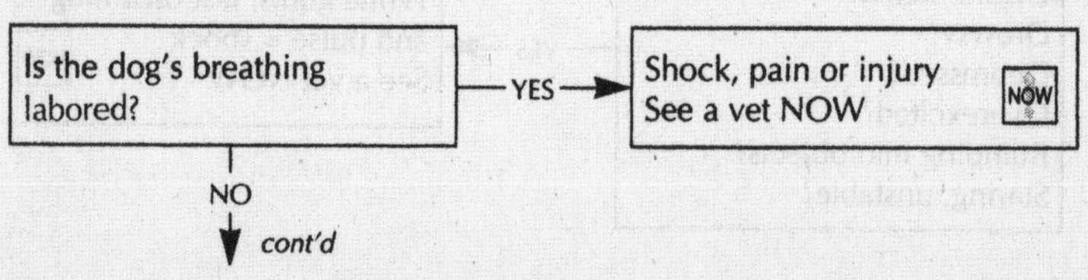
Is the dog's breathing labored?
YES
Shock, pain or injury
See a vet NOW
NOW
NO
cont'd

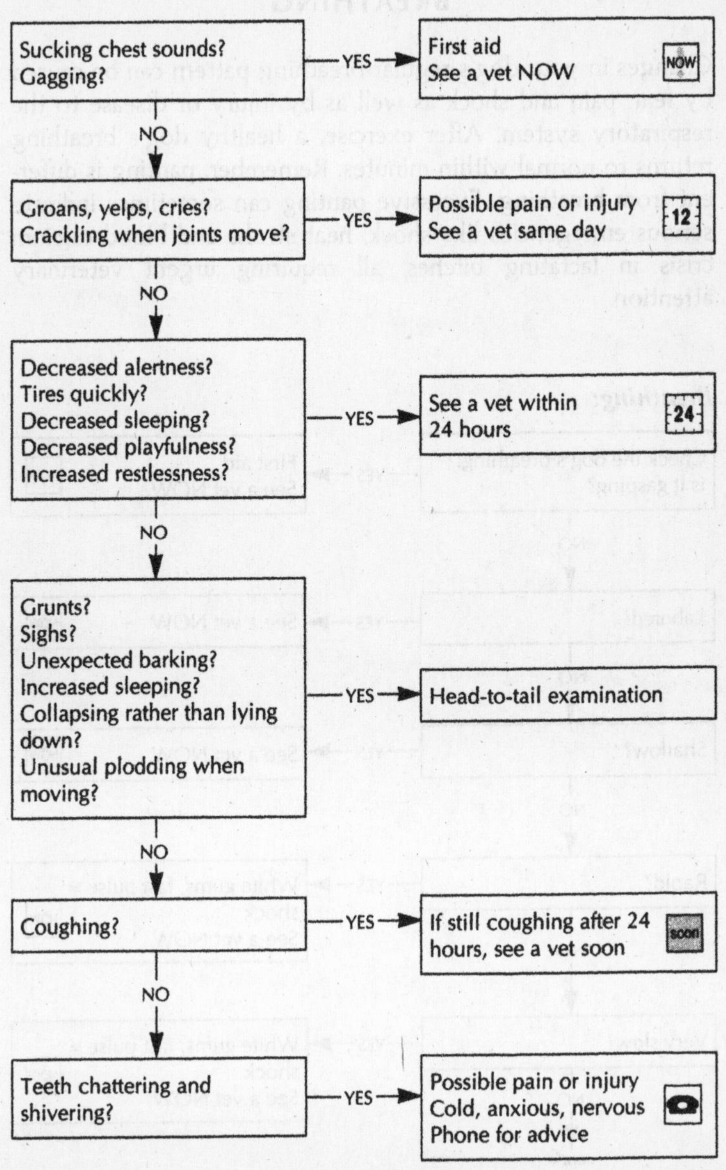
Sucking chest sounds?
Gagging?
YES
First aid
See a vet NOW
NOW
NO
Groans, yelps, cries?
Crackling when joints move?
YES
Possible pain or injury
See a vet same day
12
NO
Decreased alertness?
Tires quickly?
Decreased sleeping?
Decreased playfulness?
Increased restlessness?
YES
See a vet within
24 hours
24
NO
Grunts?
Sighs?
Unexpected barking?
Increased sleeping?
Collapsing rather than lying down?
Unusual plodding when moving?
YES
Head-to-tail examination
NO
Coughing?
YES
If still coughing after 24 hours, see a vet soon
soon
NO
Teeth chattering and shivering?
YES
Possible pain or injury
Cold, anxious, nervous
Phone for advice

BREATHING

Changes in your dog's regular breathing pattern can be caused by fear, pain and shock as well as by injury or disease to the respiratory system. After exercise, a healthy dog's breathing returns to normal within minutes. Remember, panting is different from breathing. Excessive panting can sometimes indicate serious emergencies like shock, heat stroke and blood calcium crisis in lactating bitches, all requiring urgent veterinary attention.

Breathing:

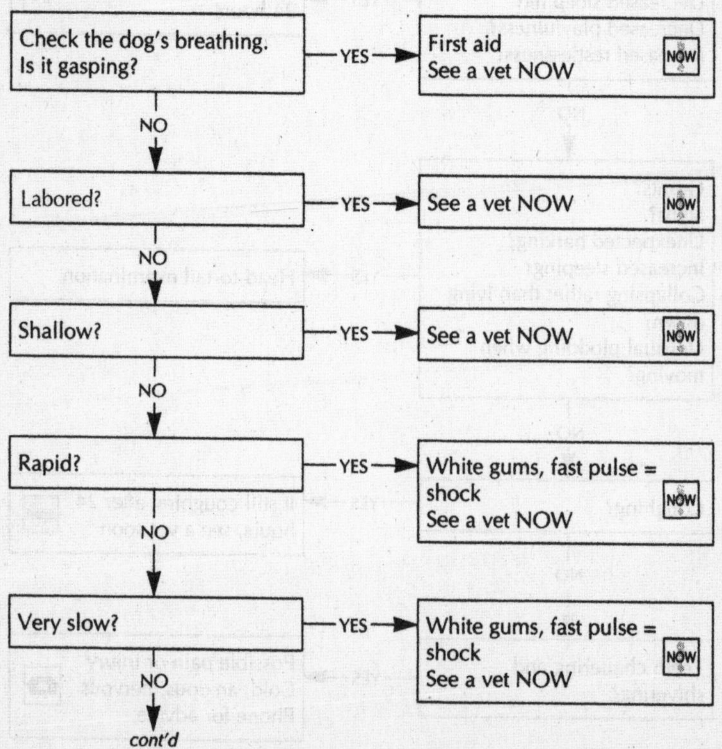
Check the dog's breathing.
Is it gasping?
YES
First aid
See a vet NOW
NOW
NO
Labored?
YES
See a vet NOW
NOW
NO
Shallow?
YES
See a vet NOW
NOW
NO
Rapid?
YES
White gums, fast pulse =
shock
See a vet NOW
NOW
NO
Very slow?
YES
White gums, fast pulse =
shock
See a vet NOW
NOW
NO
cont'd

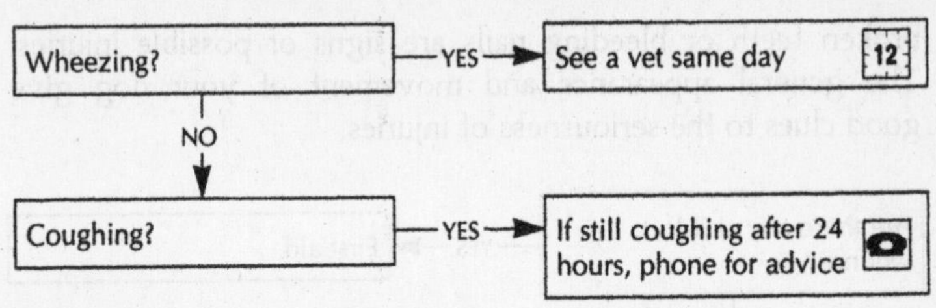
Wheezing?
YES
See a vet same day
12
NO
Coughing?
YES
If still coughing after 24 hours, phone for advice

Panting:

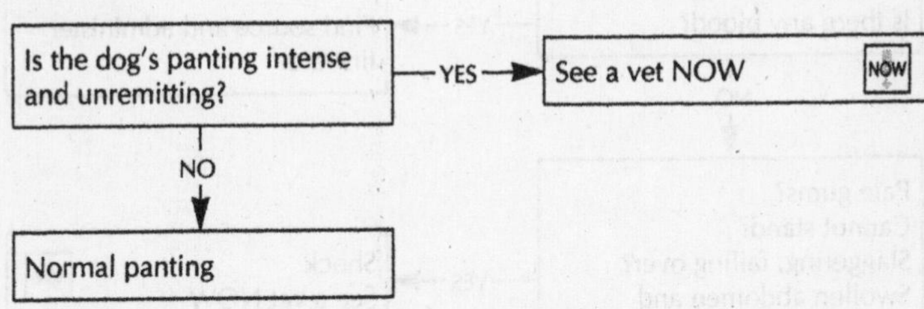
Is the dog's panting intense and unremitting?
YES
See a vet NOW
NOW
NO
Normal panting

Related behavior:

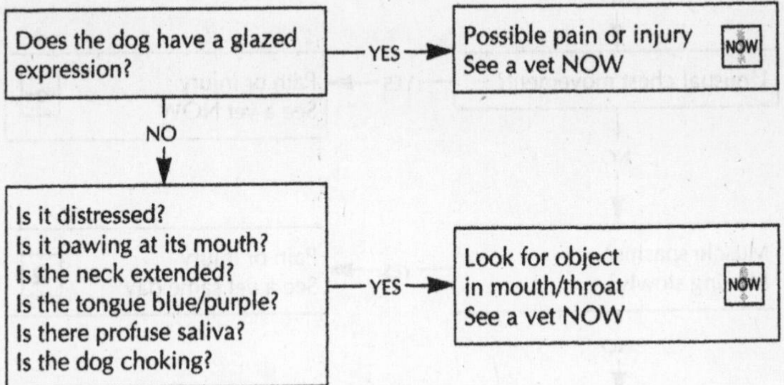
Does the dog have a glazed expression?
YES
Possible pain or injury
See a vet NOW
NOW
NO
Is it distressed?
Is it pawing at its mouth?
Is the neck extended?
Is the tongue blue/purple?
Is there profuse saliva?
Is the dog choking?
YES
Look for object in mouth/throat
See a vet NOW
NOW

GENERAL APPEARANCE AND MOVEMENT

Obvious changes in appearance such as visible wounds need immediate attention. Other changes from normal such as broken teeth or bleeding nails are signs of possible injuries. The general appearance and movement of your dog give good clues to the seriousness of injuries.

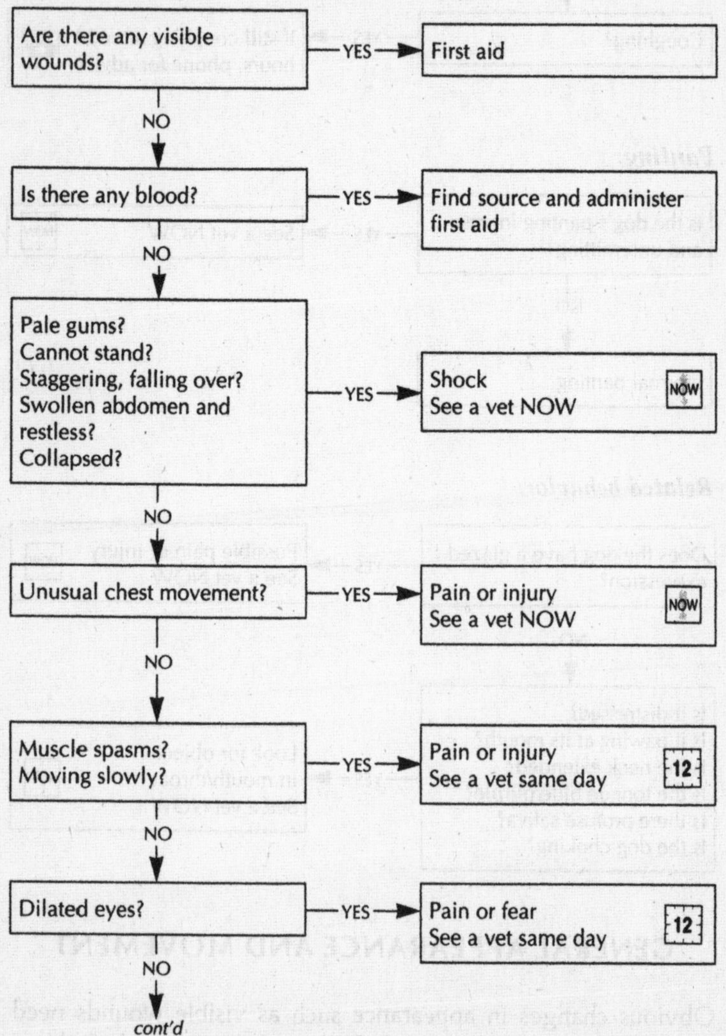
Are there any visible wounds?
YES
First aid
NO
Is there any blood?
YES
Find source and administer first aid
NO
Pale gums?
Cannot stand?
Staggering, falling over?
Swollen abdomen and restless?
Collapsed?
YES
Shock
See a vet NOW
NOW
NO
Unusual chest movement?
YES
Pain or injury
See a vet NOW
NOW
NO
Muscle spasms?
Moving slowly?
YES
Pain or injury
See a vet same day
12
NO
Dilated eyes?
YES
Pain or fear
See a vet same day
12
NO
cont'd

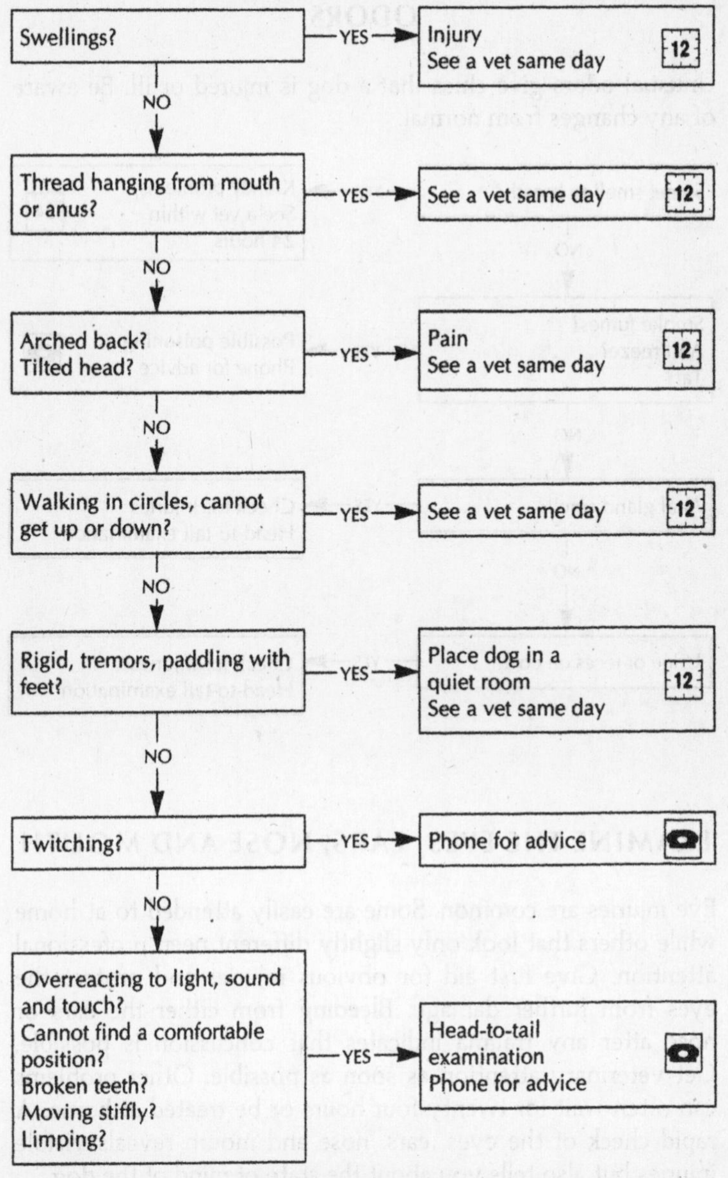
Swellings?
YES
Injury
See a vet same day
12
NO
Thread hanging from mouth or anus?
YES
See a vet same day
12
NO
Arched back?
Tilted head?
YES
Pain
See a vet same day
12
NO
Walking in circles, cannot get up or down?
YES
See a vet same day
12
NO
Rigid, tremors, paddling with feet?
YES
Place dog in a quiet room
See a vet same day
12
NO
Twitching?
YES
Phone for advice
NO
Overreacting to light, sound and touch?
Cannot find a comfortable position?
Broken teeth?
Moving stiffly?
Limping?
YES
Head-to-tail examination
Phone for advice

ODORS

Unusual odors give clues that a dog is injured or ill. Be aware of any changes from normal.

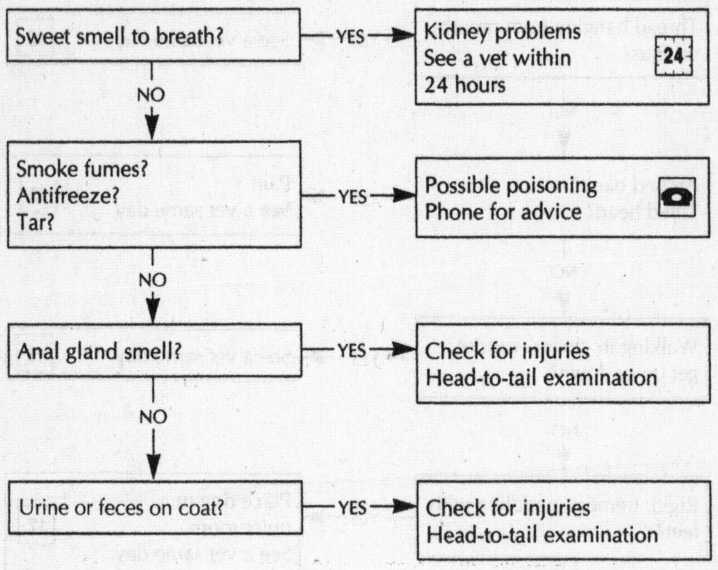
Sweet smell to breath?
YES
Kidney problems
See a vet within
24 hours
24
NO
Smoke fumes?
Antifreeze?
Tar?
YES
Possible poisoning
Phone for advice
NO
Anal gland smell?
YES
Check for injuries
Head-to-tail examination
NO
Urine or feces on coat?
YES
Check for injuries
Head-to-tail examination

EXAMINE THE EYES, EARS, NOSE AND MOUTH

Eye injuries are common. Some are easily attended to at home while others that look only slightly different need professional attention. Give first aid for obvious injuries and protect the eyes from further damage. Bleeding from either the ears or nose after any trauma indicates that concussion is possible. Get veterinary attention as soon as possible. Other problems can often wait for twenty-four hours or be treated at home. A rapid check of the eyes, ears, nose and mouth reveals visible injuries but also tells you about the state of mind of the dog.

1. Check the eyes for discharge, clouding, redness, bleeding or injuries. Dilated pupils in good light mean fear, pain, excitement or shock.
2. Test vision by flicking your finger at the eye. If your dog can see the finger it will blink. Alternatively, throw a ball of cotton in front of the dog and watch it follow the motion with its eyes.
3. Examine the ears for bleeding in the canals or external injuries. Flattened ears can mean pain, distress or weakness as well as submission.
4. Examine the nose for bleeding or discharge.
5. Check the mouth for foreign material or injuries to the tongue and hard palate. Internal mouth damage usually means there has been an injury at speed, for example a car accident or a fall.

EYES

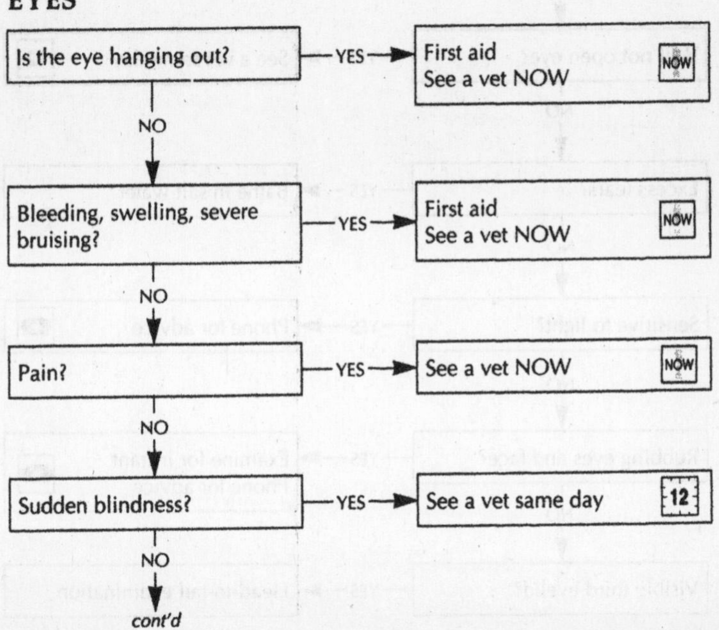
Is the eye hanging out?
YES
First aid
See a vet NOW
NOW
NO
Bleeding, swelling, severe bruising?
YES
First aid
See a vet NOW
NOW
NO
Pain?
YES
See a vet NOW
NOW
NO
Sudden blindness?
YES
See a vet same day
12
NO
cont'd

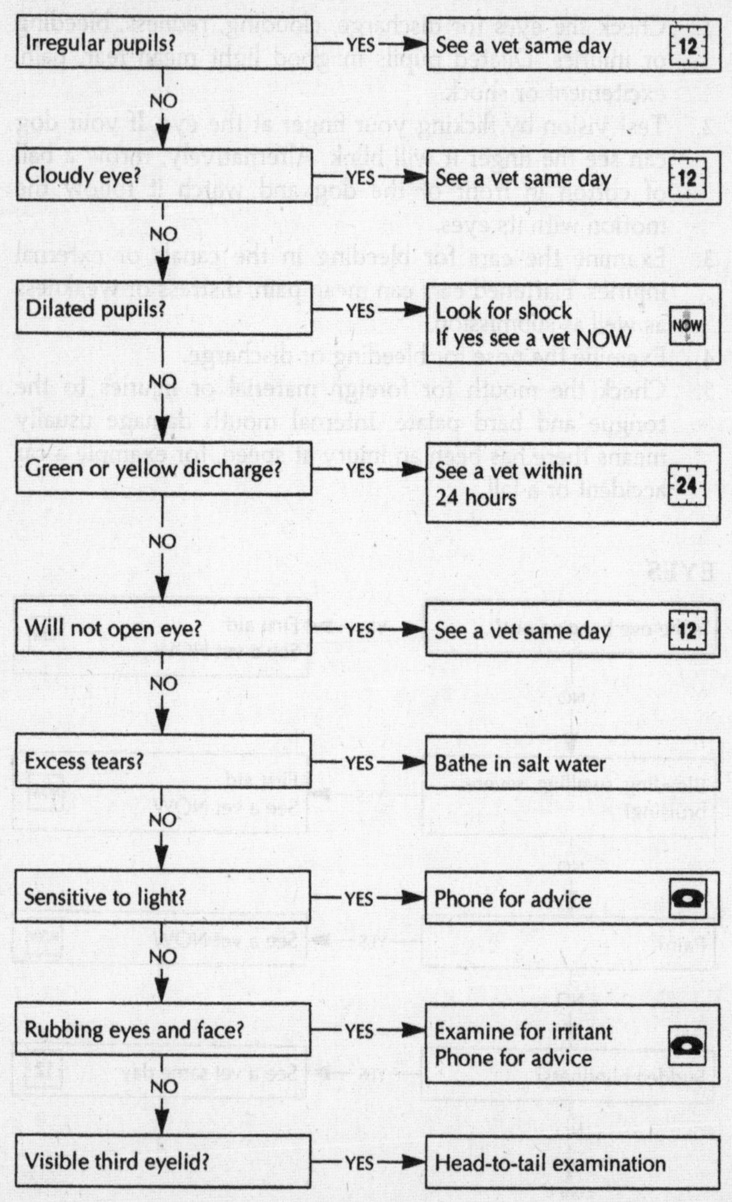
Irregular pupils?
YES
See a vet same day
12
NO
Cloudy eye?
YES
See a vet same day
12
NO
Dilated pupils?
YES
Look for shock
If yes see a vet NOW
NOW
NO
Green or yellow discharge?
YES
See a vet within
24 hours
24
NO
Will not open eye?
YES
See a vet same day
12
NO
Excess tears?
YES
Bathe in salt water
NO
Sensitive to light?
YES
Phone for advice
NO
Rubbing eyes and face?
YES
Examine for irritant
Phone for advice
NO
Visible third eyelid?
YES
Head-to-tail examination

EARS

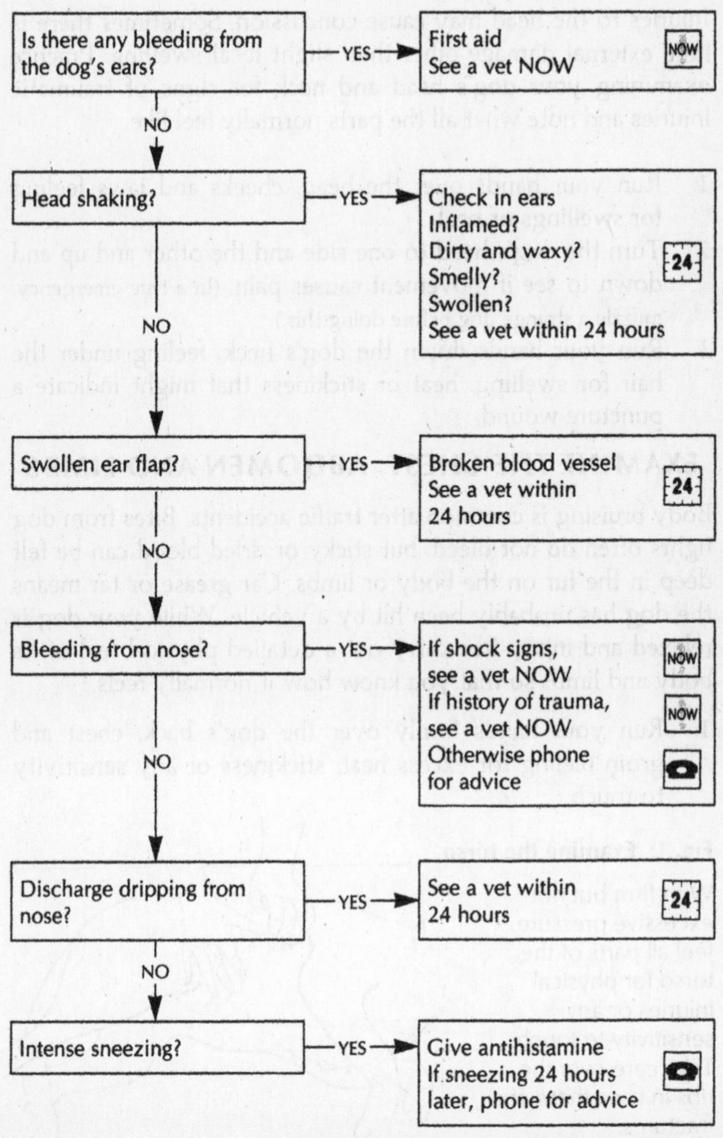
Is there any bleeding from the dog's ears?
YES
First aid
See a vet NOW
NOW
NO
Head shaking?
YES
Check in ears
Inflamed?
Dirty and waxy?
Smelly?
Swollen?
See a vet within 24 hours
24
NO
Swollen ear flap?
YES
Broken blood vessel
See a vet within
24 hours
24
NO
Bleeding from nose?
YES
If shock signs,
see a vet NOW
If history of trauma,
see a vet NOW
Otherwise phone
for advice
NOW
NOW
NO
Discharge dripping from
nose?
YES
See a vet within
24 hours
24
NO
Intense sneezing?
YES
Give antihistamine
If sneezing 24 hours
later, phone for advice

EXAMINE THE HEAD AND NECK

Injuries to the head may cause concussion. Sometimes there is little external damage other than slight local swelling. Practice examining your dog's head and neck for signs of traumatic injuries and note what all the parts normally feel like.

1. Run your hands over the head, cheeks and jaws feeling for swellings or heat.
2. Turn the dog's head to one side and the other and up and down to see if movement causes pain. (In a true emergency, muzzle a strange dog before doing this.)
3. Run your hands down the dog's neck, feeling under the hair for swelling, heat or stickiness that might indicate a puncture wound.

EXAMINE THE CHEST, ABDOMEN AND LIMBS

Body bruising is common after traffic accidents. Bites from dog fights often do not bleed, but sticky or dried blood can be felt deep in the fur on the body or limbs. Car grease or tar means the dog has probably been hit by a vehicle. While your dog is relaxed and injury-free carry out a detailed physical feel of its body and limbs so that you know how it normally feels.

1. Run your hands firmly over the dog's back, chest and groin feeling for excess heat, stickiness or any sensitivity to touch.

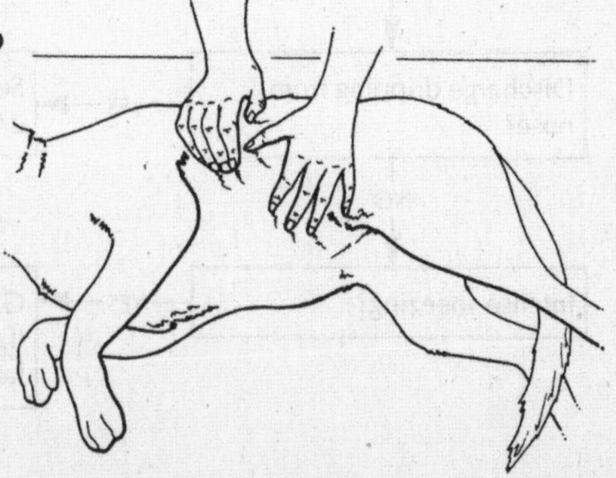

Fig. 1: Examine the torso

With firm but not excessive pressure, feel all parts of the torso for physical injuries or any sensitivity to touch. Take care over the ribs in case there are fractures.

2. Part the hair and look for skin discolouration.
3. Run your hands down each leg. Examine both forelimbs and then hind limbs together, checking for symmetry.
4. Feel each joint for excess heat or swelling.
5. Examine the paws and nails for abrasions, tears or other injuries.

EXAMINE THE TAIL, ANUS AND GENITALS

Increased sensitivity, altered odors or variation in the color or consistency of body waste are all clues to potential internal injuries or disease. Examine your dog's tail, anus and genitals while it is free from injury or illness to recognize the normal odors and anatomy of these regions.

1. Run your hand firmly along the length of the tail. There should be no obvious bumps or areas of excess heat. (Some unneutered male dogs develop a scent marking gland at the top of the tail about 5 cm (2 inches) from the tail base. This becomes swollen and hair drops out. It does not cause a problem unless it becomes infected.)
2. If a tail hangs limp or does not wag, pinch it to see if the dog responds. (Lack of response means either a tail or spinal injury.)
3. Lift the dog's tail. The anal region should be clean with no signs of clinging waste. An intense and offensive smell means that the dog has emptied its anal glands. This is a clue that the dog has been frightened or injured.
4. Examine the scrotum for swelling or injuries, and the opening of the penis or vagina for inflammation or discharge.

If a normally tidy dog's coat smells of urine, this is a sign of either illness or injury.

Do not be alarmed if your male dog develops a bulb-like

swelling on his penis. This is a 'gland' that swells when he mates with a female. This swollen 'lump' is what temporarily 'ties' dogs together during mating. (If your dog gets excited and his penis becomes stuck outside its sheath, lubricate it with K-Y (water soluble) jelly. In most instances it will go down on its own within half an hour.)

SKIN AND COAT CONDITION

Skin problems seldom need immediate veterinary attention, and many can be controlled and eliminated without veterinary treatment. Others indicate that a dog has more serious internal problems.

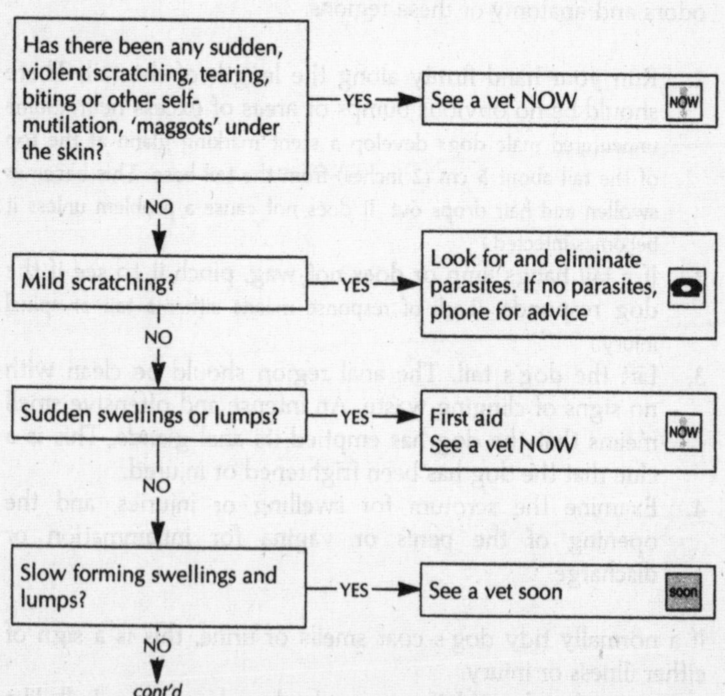
Has there been any sudden, violent scratching, tearing, biting or other self-mutilation, 'maggots' under the skin?
YES
See a vet NOW
NOW
NO
Mild scratching?
YES
Look for and eliminate parasites. If no parasites, phone for advice
NO
Sudden swellings or lumps?
YES
First aid
See a vet NOW
NOW
NO
Slow forming swellings and lumps?
YES
See a vet soon
soon
NO
cont'd

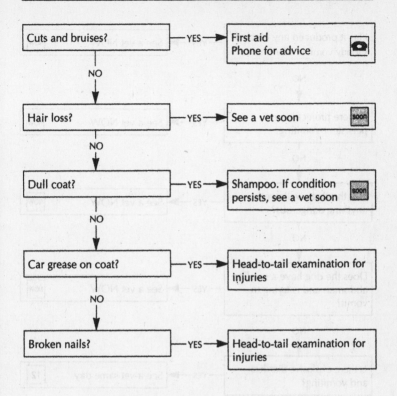

Question	If YES
Cuts and bruises?	First aid Phone for advice
Hair loss?	See a vet soon
Dull coat?	Shampoo. If condition persists, see a vet soon
Car grease on coat?	Head-to-tail examination for injuries
Broken nails?	Head-to-tail examination for injuries

GASTROINTESTINAL CHANGES

Dogs have the unfortunate habit of quite literally tasting life. This curiosity leads to many gastrointestinal emergencies, some of which need the most urgent attention. Always err on the side of caution when deciding what to do.

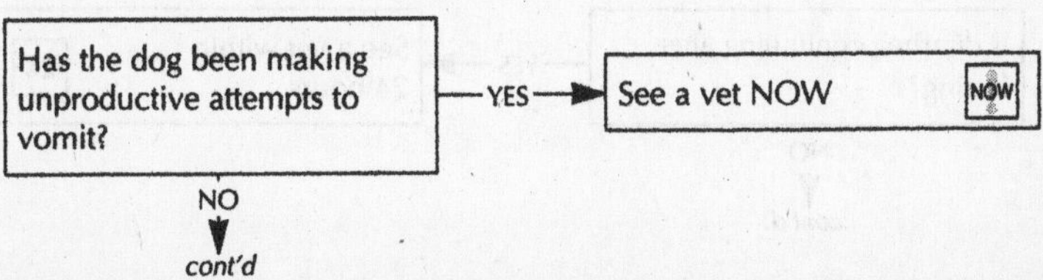
Has the dog been making unproductive attempts to vomit?
YES
See a vet NOW
NOW
NO
cont'd

GASTROINTESTINAL CHANGES

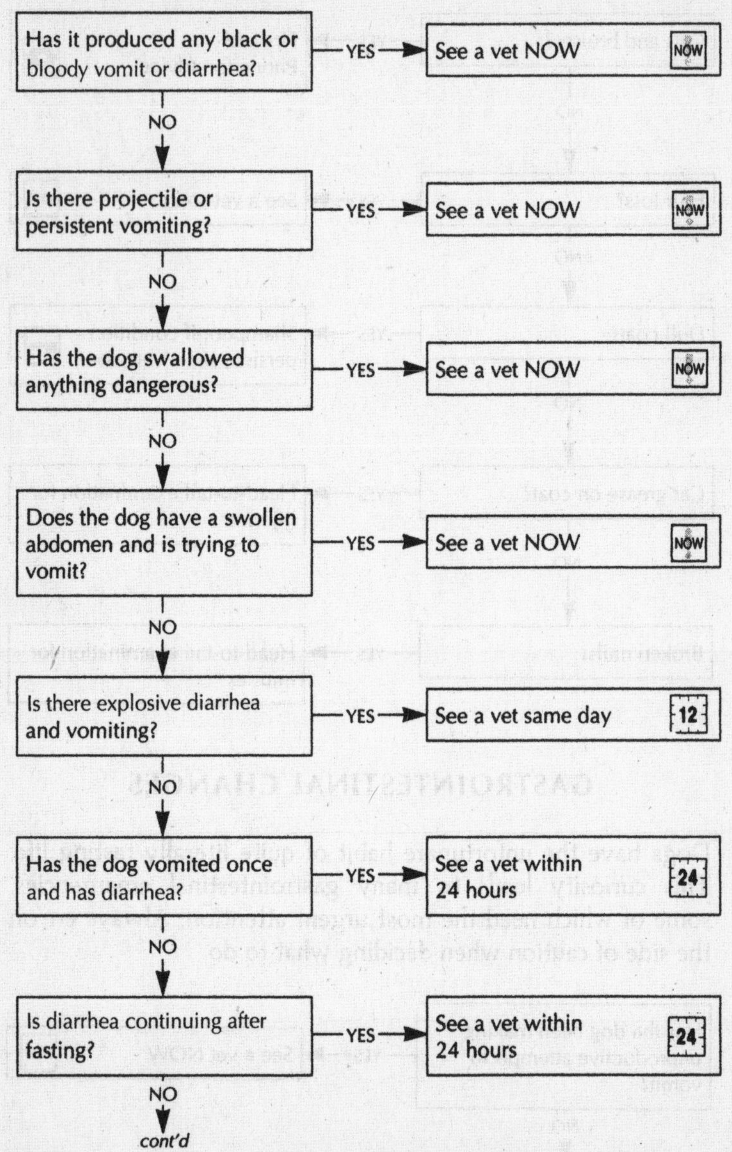

Has it produced any black or bloody vomit or diarrhea?
YES
See a vet NOW
NOW
NO
Is there projectile or persistent vomiting?
YES
See a vet NOW
NOW
NO
Has the dog swallowed anything dangerous?
YES
See a vet NOW
NOW
NO
Does the dog have a swollen abdomen and is trying to vomit?
YES
See a vet NOW
NOW
NO
Is there explosive diarrhea and vomiting?
YES
See a vet same day
12
NO
Has the dog vomited once and has diarrhea?
YES
See a vet within 24 hours
24
NO
Is diarrhea continuing after fasting?
YES
See a vet within 24 hours
24
NO
cont'd

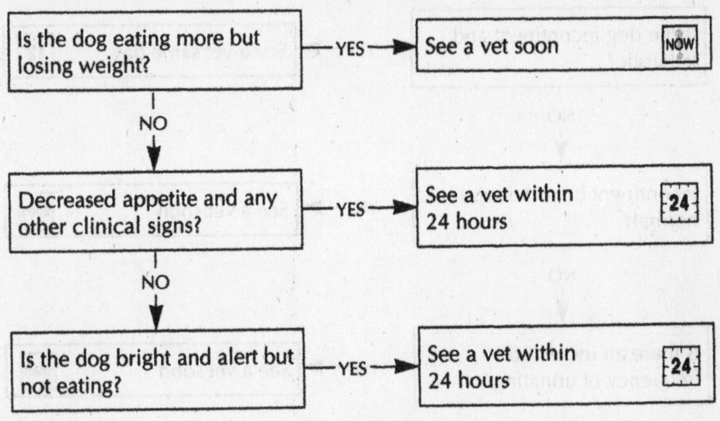
Is the dog eating more but losing weight?
YES
See a vet soon
NOW
NO
Decreased appetite and any other clinical signs?
YES
See a vet within 24 hours
24
NO
Is the dog bright and alert but not eating?
YES
See a vet within 24 hours
24

TOILET HABITS

Changes in a dog's sanitary habits are often indicators that medical attention is needed. Some changes require immediate attention while others can wait twenty-four hours or longer.

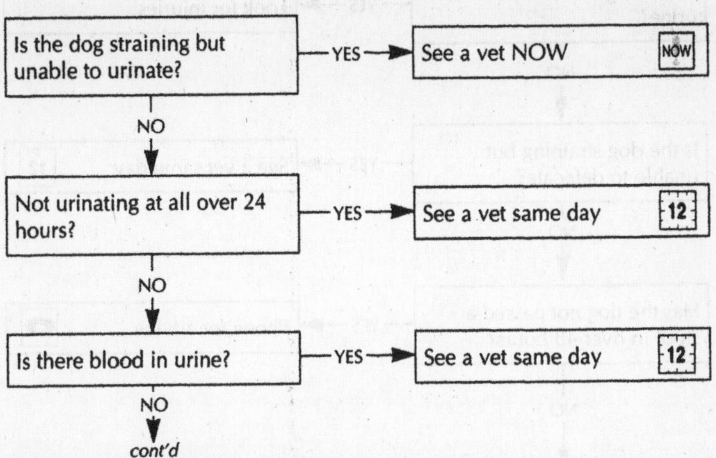
Is the dog straining but unable to urinate?
YES
See a vet NOW
NOW
NO
Not urinating at all over 24 hours?
YES
See a vet same day
12
NO
Is there blood in urine?
YES
See a vet same day
12
NO
cont'd

TOILET HABITS

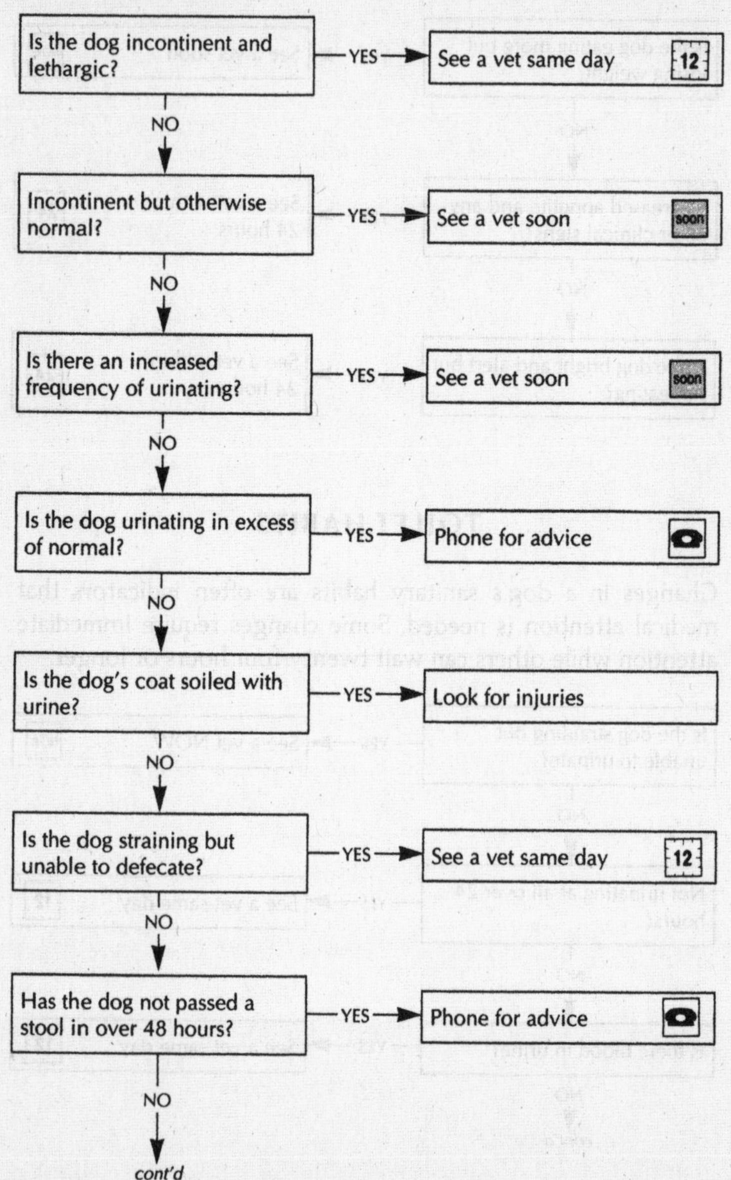

Is the dog incontinent and lethargic?
YES
See a vet same day
12
NO
Incontinent but otherwise normal?
YES
See a vet soon
soon
NO
Is there an increased frequency of urinating?
YES
See a vet soon
soon
NO
Is the dog urinating in excess of normal?
YES
Phone for advice
NO
Is the dog's coat soiled with urine?
YES
Look for injuries
NO
Is the dog straining but unable to defecate?
YES
See a vet same day
12
NO
Has the dog not passed a stool in over 48 hours?
YES
Phone for advice
NO
cont'd

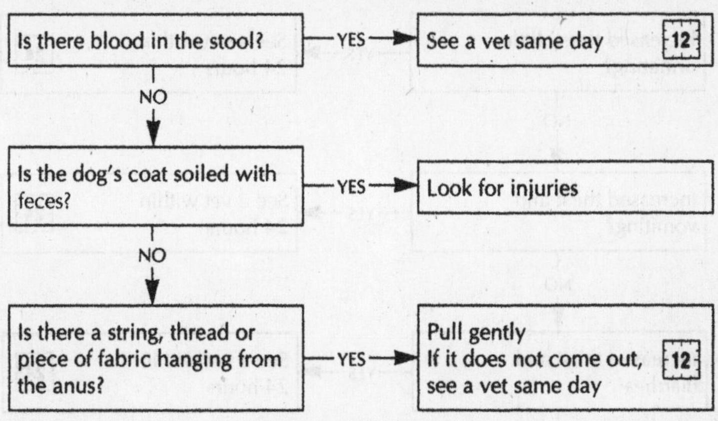
Is there blood in the stool?
YES
See a vet same day
12
NO
Is the dog's coat soiled with feces?
YES
Look for injuries
NO
Is there a string, thread or piece of fabric hanging from the anus?
YES
Pull gently
If it does not come out, see a vet same day
12

CHANGES IN DRINKING AND URINATING

Increased thirst often indicates significant medical problems. Some of these need urgent attention.

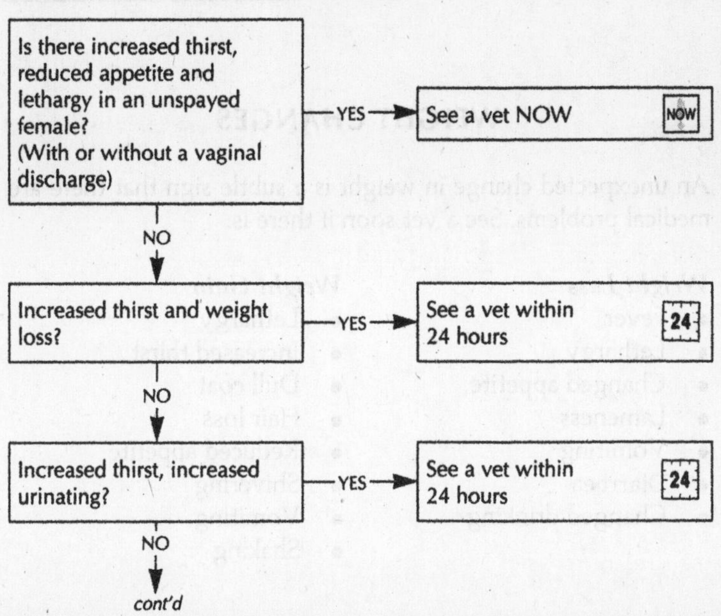
Is there increased thirst, reduced appetite and lethargy in an unspayed female?
(With or without a vaginal discharge)
YES
See a vet NOW
NOW
NO
Increased thirst and weight loss?
YES
See a vet within 24 hours
24
NO
Increased thirst, increased urinating?
YES
See a vet within 24 hours
24
NO
cont'd

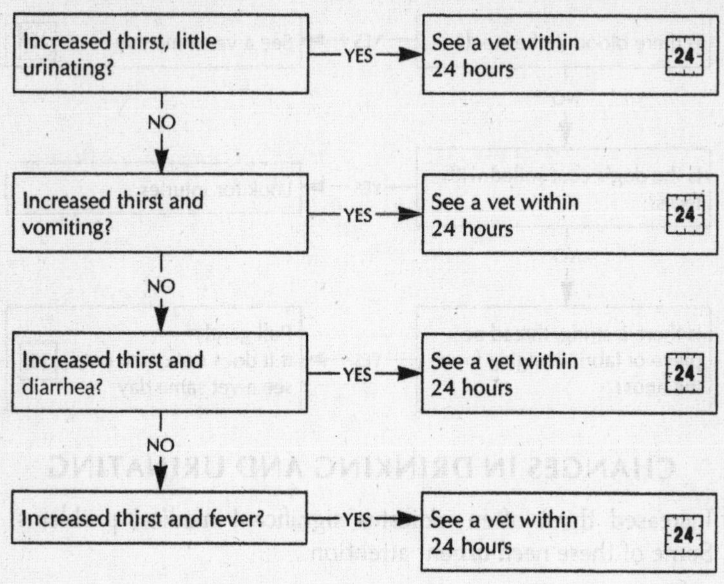
Increased thirst, little urinating?
YES
See a vet within 24 hours
24
NO
Increased thirst and vomiting?
YES
See a vet within 24 hours
24
NO
Increased thirst and diarrhea?
YES
See a vet within 24 hours
24
NO
Increased thirst and fever?
YES
See a vet within 24 hours
24

WEIGHT CHANGES

An unexpected change in weight is a subtle sign that there are medical problems. See a vet soon if there is:

Weight Loss

- Fever
- Lethargy
- Changed appetite
- Lameness
- Vomiting
- Diarrhea
- Changed drinking

Weight Gain

- Lethargy
- Increased thirst
- Dull coat
- Hair loss
- Reduced appetite
- Shivering
- Vomiting
- Shaking

PART THREE

EMERGENCIES

Principles of First Aid

Follow these simple principles when faced with a canine emergency:

- **Do not panic**
  Stay calm. The dog's life may depend upon your common sense.
- **Assess the situation**
  What has happened?
- **Are you in danger?**
  Do not take foolish risks.
- **Is the dog in further danger?**
  Carefully move the dog if it is safe to do so.
- **Assess the dog's condition**
  Is it conscious or unconscious? Do not waste time with a detailed examination or diagnosis until immediate problems are treated.
- **Give emergency first aid**
  Give artificial respiration and heart massage if necessary.
- **Get help if necessary or available**
  When possible, one person organizes equipment and transport while the other tends to the injured dog.

- **Transport the dog to the vet**
- **Watch for shock**

  Regardless of its specific cause, shock is the most likely life threatening emergency you will encounter.

> **WATCH FOR SHOCK**
>
> **Pale or white gums, rapid breathing, weak and rapid pulse, cold extremities, general weakness.**
>
> (For treatment of shock see under **Shock** on page 10.)

How to Use This Part

In this part the most likely emergencies are listed in alphabetical order. If your dog is ill or injured, decide what the most important clinical sign is: burns, eye injuries, poisons, scratching, etc., then look under the appropriate heading. Alternatively, look in the index at the end of the book to find the section you need.

This part describes most of the common emergencies you will encounter. For each emergency there is a short **description** of the signs of the injury or illness and then **illustrated instructions** showing what to do.

Deciding whether your dog needs veterinary attention and, if so, when, can be difficult. For each emergency there is a **decision chart** to help you decide what to do after you have provided first aid. For a full explanation of the symbols and information in the decision charts, see under **Deciding If and When Your Dog Needs Veterinary Attention** on page 37.

Be thorough. Record signs and symptoms as they occur. Details such as water intake and frequency or absence of bowel movements are beneficial to your veterinarian.

Remember, the most common preventable mistake made by pet owners prior to arriving at the vet's with an emergency is failure to seek veterinary advice sooner. Do not make this unfortunate mistake. If you are not absolutely certain that you know what has happened and can handle the emergency yourself, call your vet immediately. It only costs the price of a phone call.

Immediate First Aid for the Conscious Dog

When emergencies happen, remember to assess the situation and the dog's condition. Do not get diverted by obvious injuries such as minor cuts and wounds. Restrain the dog when necessary, look for signs of shock, check the dog for any life threatening signs then carry out any necessary minor first aid.

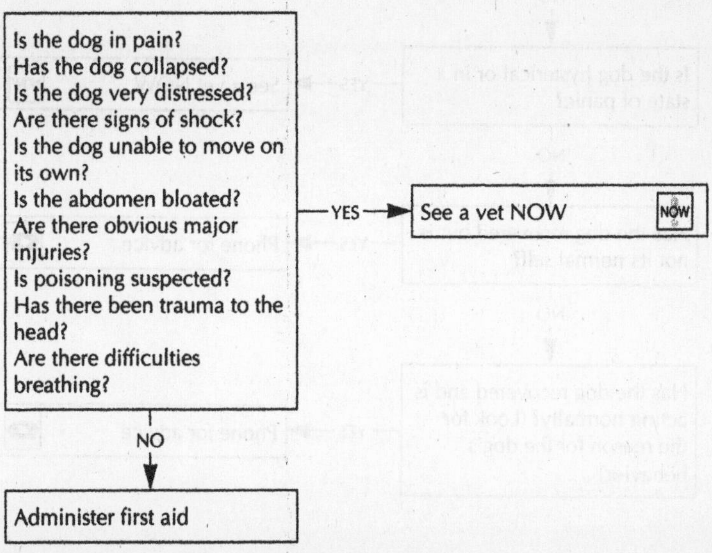
Is the dog in pain?
Has the dog collapsed?
Is the dog very distressed?
Are there signs of shock?
Is the dog unable to move on its own?
Is the abdomen bloated?
Are there obvious major injuries?
Is poisoning suspected?
Has there been trauma to the head?
Are there difficulties breathing?
YES
See a vet NOW
NOW
NO
Administer first aid

If there are potentially life threatening situations see your veterinarian immediately. Otherwise, provide first aid and follow the advice in the decision charts.

AGGRESSION AND BEHAVIOR CHANGES

Aggression is perfectly normal under many circumstances. However, it is also a sign of illness or disease. Unexpected aggression from a normally placid and amenable dog can be caused by pain, fever, brain damage (including tumors), infections (including rabies), head wounds, convulsions and seizures, diabetic crisis and other conditions, including panic attacks, that require veterinary attention. If your dog suddenly becomes aggressive, consider the following:

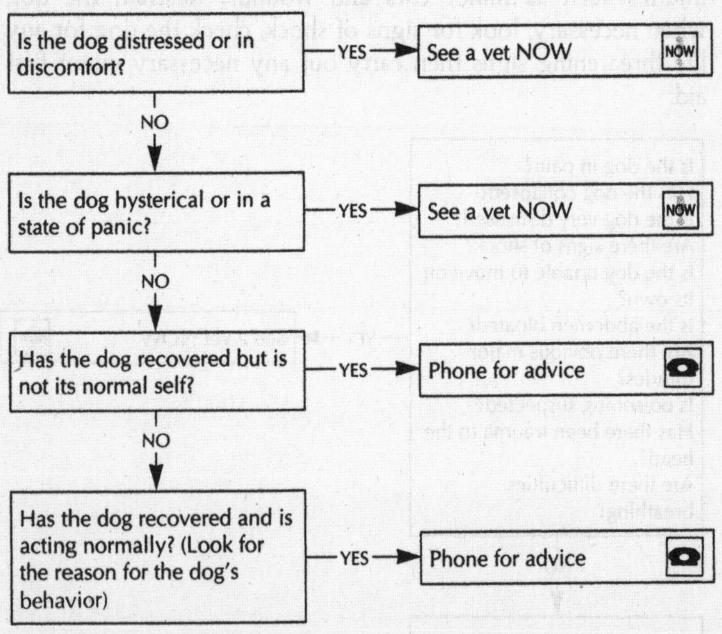
Is the dog distressed or in discomfort?
YES
See a vet NOW
NOW
NO
Is the dog hysterical or in a state of panic?
YES
See a vet NOW
NOW
NO
Has the dog recovered but is not its normal self?
YES
Phone for advice
NO
Has the dog recovered and is acting normally? (Look for the reason for the dog's behavior)
YES
Phone for advice

1. Protect yourself, other people and other animals from bites.
2. Reduce sensory stimulation by eliminating noise and light.
3. When your dog has become calmer, speak to it soothingly. If it responds to normal commands, attach a lead to the collar and leave it on. This enables you to control the dog more easily if it suddenly becomes aggressive again.
4. If the dog does not calm down, in the absence of the risk of rabies, throw a blanket over it and take it to the vet. When rabies is a possible cause of the behavior change, telephone for professional assistance from your veterinarian or animal control agency (dog wardens, ASPCA or police).

BIRTH

Difficulties at birth can be caused by a narrow birth canal, weak contractions or abnormalities to the fetus. Breeds with large heads compared to the size of their bodies, like bulldogs, are prone to problems. Older, overweight and nervous bitches are more likely to suffer from weak contractions than others.

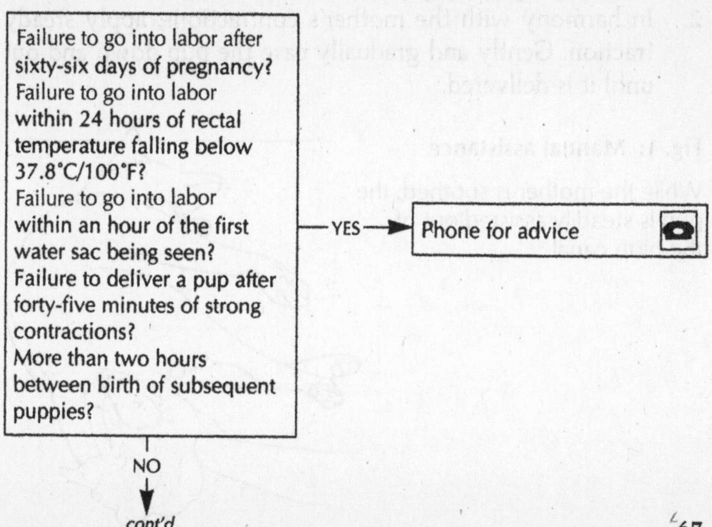
Failure to go into labor after sixty-six days of pregnancy?
Failure to go into labor within 24 hours of rectal temperature falling below 37.8°C/100°F?
Failure to go into labor within an hour of the first water sac being seen?
Failure to deliver a pup after forty-five minutes of strong contractions?
More than two hours between birth of subsequent puppies?
YES
Phone for advice
NO
cont'd

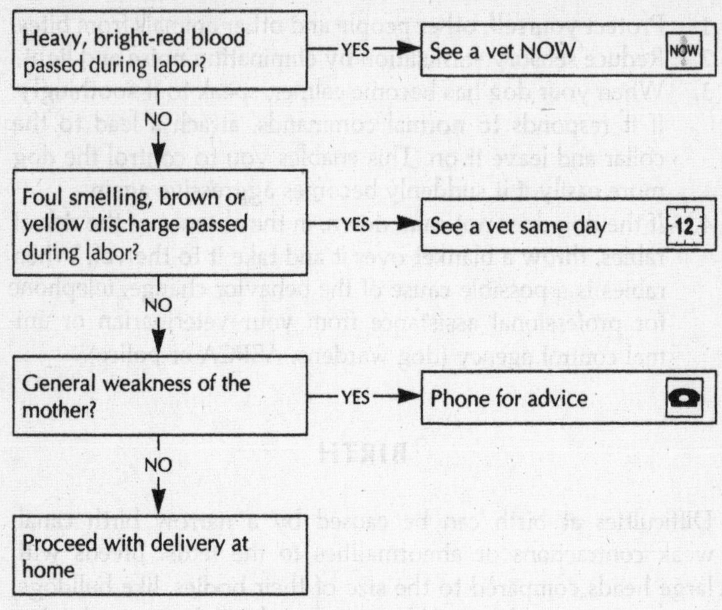
Heavy, bright-red blood passed during labor?
YES
See a vet NOW
NOW
NO
Foul smelling, brown or yellow discharge passed during labor?
YES
See a vet same day
12
NO
General weakness of the mother?
YES
Phone for advice
NO
Proceed with delivery at home

If a pup is stuck in the birth canal:

1. Gently grasp the pup with a warm, clean towel.
2. In harmony with the mother's contractions, apply steady traction. Gently and gradually ease the pup down and out until it is delivered.

Fig. 1: Manual assistance

While the mother is soothed, the pup is steadily assisted out of the birth canal.

3. If you cannot get the pup out, see your veterinarian immediately.

If the mother does not show interest in the pup:

1. Place the newborn pup on a warm, clean towel.
2. Using the towel, peel the membranes from around the pup's head then off the body. The membranes will gather around the umbilical cord. (Do not pull on or cut the cord.)

Fig. 2: The membranes are removed

The mouth and nostrils are cleared of fluid making it possible for the pup to breathe.

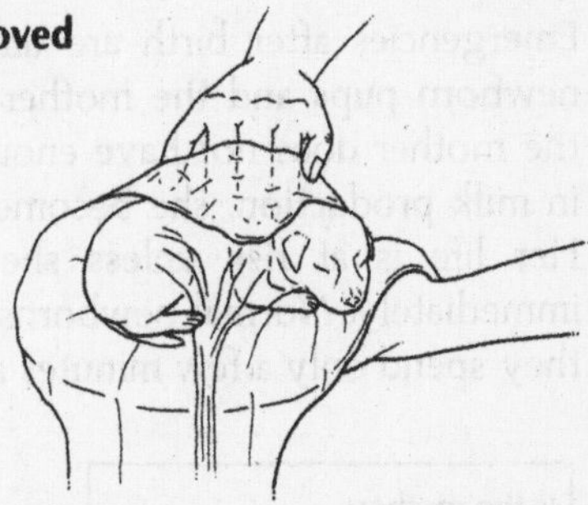

3. After wiping fluid from the pup's face, rub its body with the towel vigorously to stimulate breathing.
4. If the pup does not breathe, cradle it in the towel between your cupped hands. Raise your hands to shoulder height then swing them down rapidly in an arc to expel fluid from the air passages. Repeat this several times.

Fig. 3: Expel fluid from air passages

Hold the pup firmly while swinging your cupped hands in an arc, then remove expelled fluid from the nose and mouth.

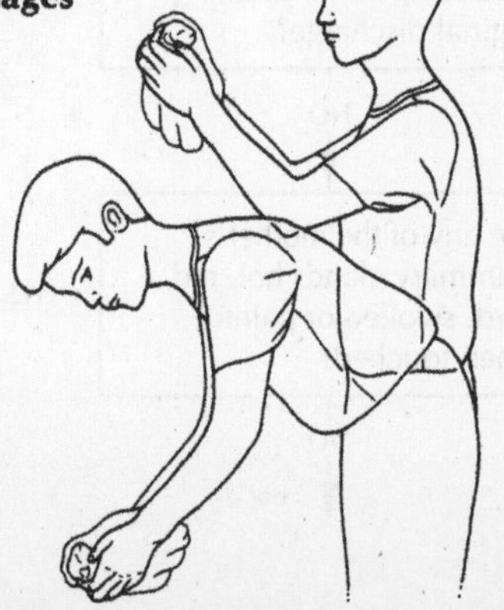

5. Rub the pup vigorously with the towel. Stop treatment when it actively breathes, cries or moves.
6. Return the pup to its mother. If she is unwilling to care for it, contact your veterinarian. (If the mother does not chew off the afterbirth, tie a thread round each umbilical cord about 2.5 cm (1 inch) from the pup's abdomen. Cut off the afterbirth, leaving the tied thread on the portion attached to the pup.)

AFTER BIRTH

Emergencies after birth are unlikely but can occur. Both the newborn pups and the mother are susceptible to infection. If the mother does not have enough calcium in her body to use in milk production, she becomes agitated and pants intensely. Her life is at risk unless she receives intravenous calcium immediately. Normal newborns are either sleeping or nursing, they spend only a few minutes a day moving or vocalizing.

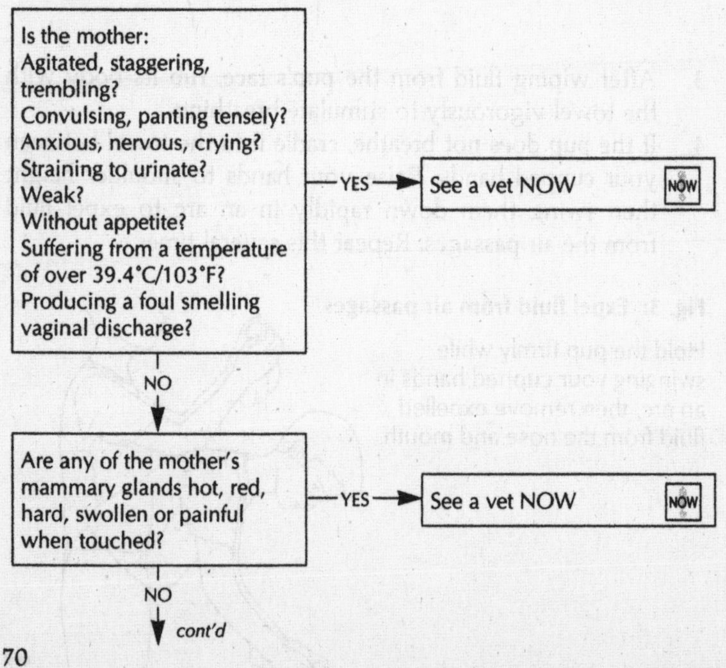
Is the mother:
Agitated, staggering, trembling?
Convulsing, panting tensely?
Anxious, nervous, crying?
Straining to urinate?
Weak?
Without appetite?
Suffering from a temperature of over 39.4°C/103°F?
Producing a foul smelling vaginal discharge?
YES
See a vet NOW
NOW
NO
Are any of the mother's mammary glands hot, red, hard, swollen or painful when touched?
YES
See a vet NOW
NOW
NO
cont'd

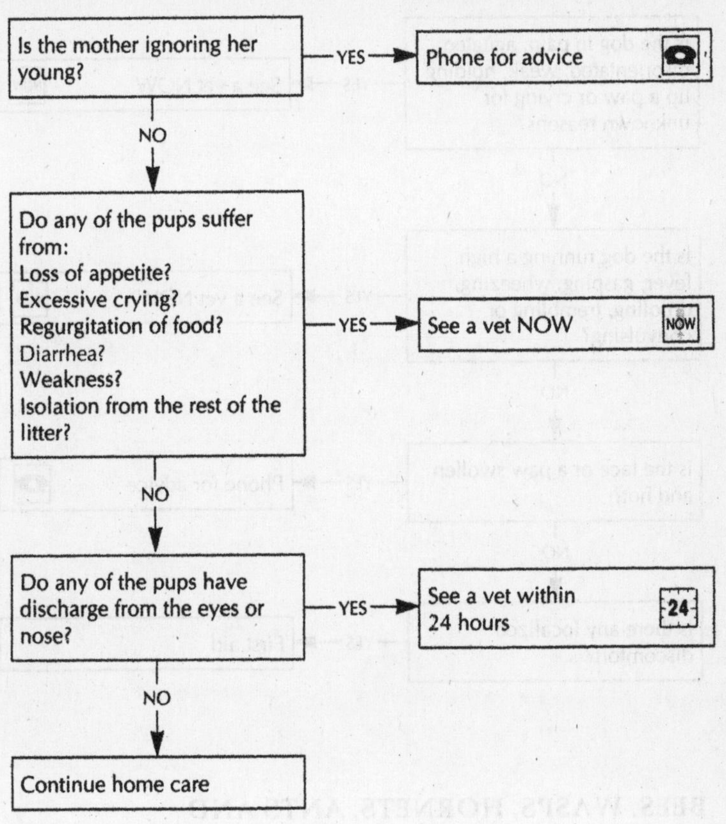
Is the mother ignoring her young?
YES
Phone for advice
NO
Do any of the pups suffer from:
Loss of appetite?
Excessive crying?
Regurgitation of food?
Diarrhea?
Weakness?
Isolation from the rest of the litter?
YES
See a vet NOW
NOW
NO
Do any of the pups have discharge from the eyes or nose?
YES
See a vet within 24 hours
24
NO
Continue home care

BITES AND STINGS

Bites and stings often occur unseen. The dog returns showing signs of discomfort or distress.

Animal bites are covered under **Puncture wounds** on page 156.

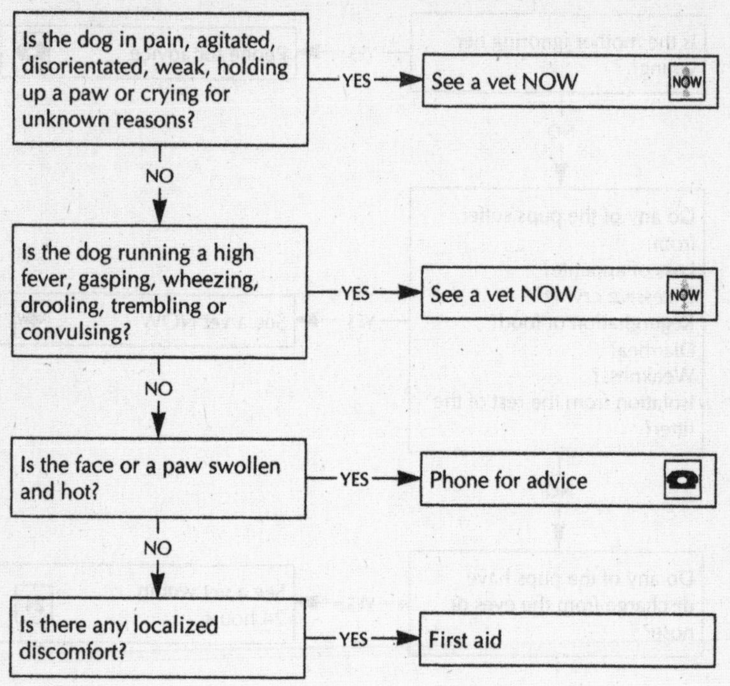
Is the dog in pain, agitated, disorientated, weak, holding up a paw or crying for unknown reasons?
YES
See a vet NOW
NOW
NO
Is the dog running a high fever, gasping, wheezing, drooling, trembling or convulsing?
YES
See a vet NOW
NOW
NO
Is the face or a paw swollen and hot?
YES
Phone for advice
NO
Is there any localized discomfort?
YES
First aid

BEES, WASPS, HORNETS, ANTS AND CATERPILLARS

Stings and bites from bees, wasps, hornets and ants usually cause only local irritation and relatively harmless reactions. Some dogs suffer from more acute and life threatening allergic reactions that need immediate veterinary treatment. Contact with some types of caterpillar causes intense local itch and irritation.

The signs of local reaction are: pain, itching and swelling in an area that has been stung.

The signs of more serious reaction are: difficulty breathing, shock, vomiting, diarrhea and coma.

First aid for local reactions:

1. When possible, remove embedded stingers with tweezers or by scraping the area with a credit card. (Do not squeeze the embedded stinger. This may release further irritant.)

Fig. 1: The stinger is removed

The dog is restrained and the stinger removed by scraping the skin with a credit card.

CREDIT
CARD

2. Apply a cold pack to the swollen area.
3. Give a non-prescription antihistamine tablet.

First aid for severe reactions:

1. Get veterinary attention as quickly as possible. (The air passages may be swollen. It might be impossible to inflate the lungs with artificial respiration alone.)
2. Give CPR if the heart has stopped.
3. Give artificial respiration if breathing has stopped.
4. Treat for shock. (Severe reactions do not respond to first aid. Adrenalin and cortisone are necessary to reverse the allergic reaction.)

POISONOUS SNAKES, SPIDERS, SCORPIONS

Poisonous snakes (adders in the UK, rattlesnakes in Canada, copperheads and cottonmouths in the USA) bite dogs far more frequently than they bite humans. It is unusual to see a dog actually being bitten.

The signs of a poisonous snakebite are: trembling, excitement, vomiting, collapse, drooling, dilated pupils, fast pulse.

Poisonous spiders rarely bite dogs because spiders' mouth parts can only pierce thin skin, like the skin between the toes. Bites are a potential worry only where poisonous spiders exist such as Australia and the USA.

The signs of a poisonous spider bite are: severe pain at the site of the bite (usually the paw), drooling, vomiting, convulsions, muscle spasms and breathing difficulties.

Scorpions sting inquisitive dogs with the venom in the last segment of the tail. There is a hazard to dogs in parts of Arizona and New Mexico.

The signs of a scorpion sting are: severe pain at the site of the bite (usually the paw), drooling, general weakness, breathing difficulties and paralysis.

First aid for snake, spider and scorpion bites:

1. Minimize the dog's movement. (Excess movement speeds the poison through the body.)
2. If the bite wound is visible, wash it thoroughly with cold water to get rid of any surface venom. (Do not cut the wound or attempt to suck out venom. This increases the blood supply and makes the condition worse.)
3. If a leg is bitten, keep it below the heart, apply an ice pack (a bag of frozen vegetables) and bandage it, wrapping large sheets of cotton wool tightly around the limb and covering this with firm elastic adhesive bandage. (Tourniquets are not as effective as bandages in slowing the spread of poison.)

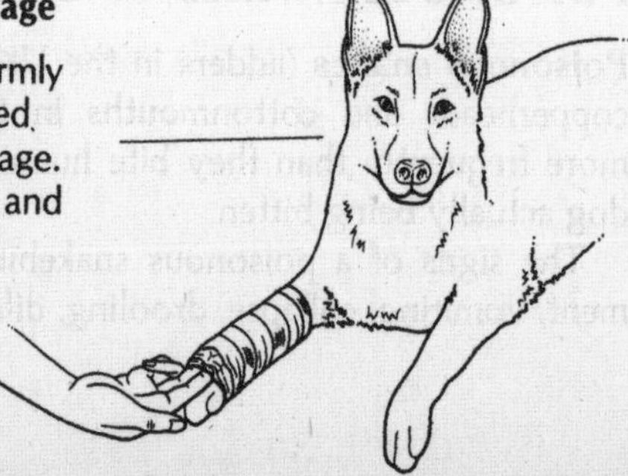

Fig. 2: Apply a thick bandage

Cotton wool is wrapped firmly around the leg then covered with elastic adhesive bandage. This minimizes movement and the spread of venom.

4. Keep the dog calm and see a local veterinarian immediately. When given promptly, anti-venom and cortisone save lives.

POISONOUS TICKS

Some **ticks** in Australia, the USA and Canada produce a toxin that causes paralysis and death. In the UK there have been confirmed reports of disease transmitted by ticks that causes depression, fever and weakness. The tick must be attached to the dog for two days before infection occurs.

The signs of tick paralysis are: fever, incoordination and weakness. The signs of other diseases transmitted by ticks include: fever, weakness, swollen and painful joints, a reluctance to move and water retention.

First aid for tick infestation:

1. Comb through the dog's fur with your fingertips.
2. Remove ticks by inverting a small container of alcohol or methylated spirit over the tick. This kills the tick. (Do not squeeze the tick. Squeezing may cause more poison to be injected into the dog.)
3. With tweezers, gently twist the mouth piece to remove the tick from the dog's skin.

JELLYFISH

Jellyfish stings are every bit as painful for dogs as they are for humans.

The signs of stings in a dog that has been swimming in the sea are: agitation, restlessness, crying and breathing difficulties.

First aid for jellyfish stings:

1. Examine the dog closely, looking for any jellyfish tentacles clinging to the fur.

2. Remove the tentacles. Wear rubber gloves if possible, as the tentacle tips can still sting you.
3. Apply dilute ammonia (one part ammonia to ten parts water) to the affected areas.
4. If the dog has no history of reactions to the drug, give aspirin by mouth in a small amount of food at a dose rate of one regular tablet per 30 Kg (66 lb) body weight.

BLEEDING

External bleeding is obvious, but **internal bleeding** – though less obvious – is equally important. If your dog has had a major injury or is acting in a subdued manner, look for signs of shock.

Spurting blood means an artery has been cut. It may be more difficult to stop arterial bleeding but once the severed vessel is located, applying firm, direct pressure can stop the bleeding immediately.

WATCH FOR SHOCK

Pale or white gums, rapid breathing, weak and rapid pulse, cold extremities, general weakness.

(For treatment of shock see under **Shock** on page 10.)

Cleaning and bandaging wounds is covered on pages 19–25.

INTERNAL BLEEDING

1. If the dog has collapsed, place it on its side with the head extended.
2. Elevate the hindquarters using a folded blanket, towel or pillow.

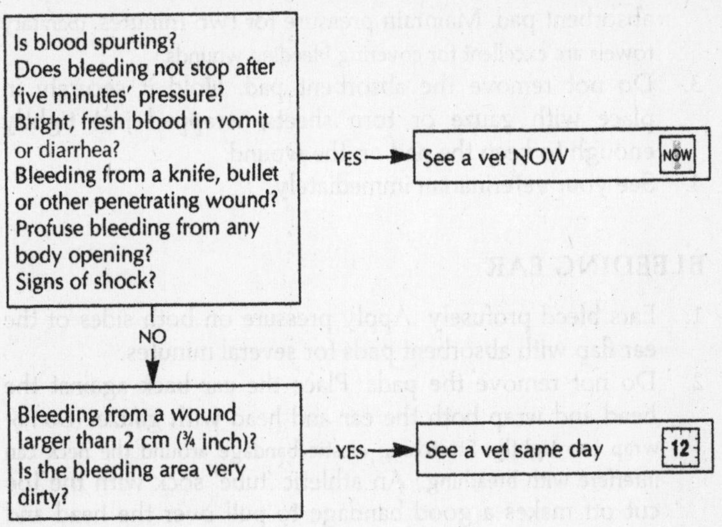
Is blood spurting?
Does bleeding not stop after five minutes' pressure?
Bright, fresh blood in vomit or diarrhea?
Bleeding from a knife, bullet or other penetrating wound?
Profuse bleeding from any body opening?
Signs of shock?
YES
See a vet NOW
NOW
NO
Bleeding from a wound larger than 2 cm (¾ inch)?
Is the bleeding area very dirty?
YES
See a vet same day
12

Fig. 1: Treat for shock

The hindquarters are elevated, a wrapped hot water bottle provides extra warmth and the dog is covered in blankets while it is taken as quickly as possible to the veterinarian.

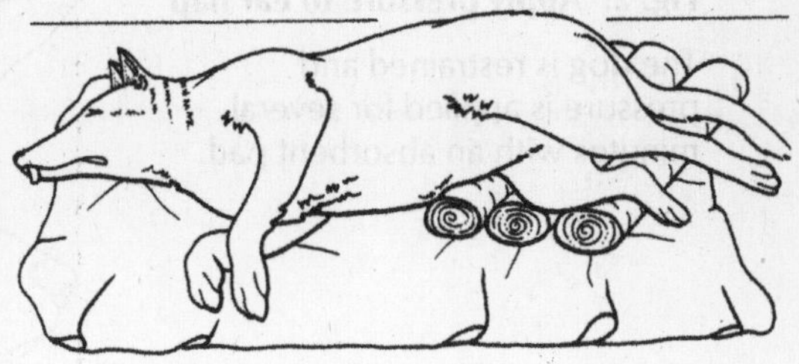

3. Wrap the dog in coats or blankets and take to the veterinarian immediately.

BLEEDING FROM THE HEAD AND TORSO

1. Restrain the dog.
2. Clean minor wounds. Apply pressure immediately to more severe bleeding by covering the wound with an

absorbent pad. Maintain pressure for two minutes. (Sanitary towels are excellent for covering bleeding wounds.)

3. Do not remove the absorbent pad. Hold it securely in place with gauze or torn sheets, wrapped just tightly enough to keep the pad on the wound.
4. See your veterinarian immediately.

BLEEDING EAR

1. Ears bleed profusely. Apply pressure on both sides of the ear flap with absorbent pads for several minutes.
2. Do not remove the pads. Place the ear back against the head and wrap both the ear and head with gauze. (Do not wrap too tightly. Stretching elastic bandage around the neck can interfere with breathing.) An athletic 'tube' sock with the toe cut off makes a good bandage to pull over the head and hold the injured ear in place.

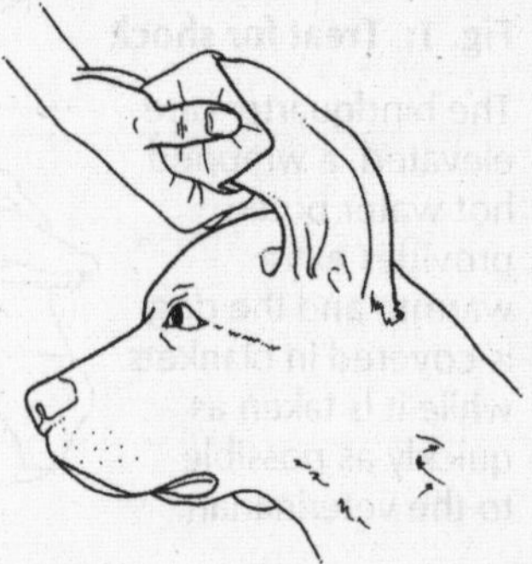

Fig. 2: Apply pressure to ear flap

The dog is restrained and pressure is applied for several minutes with an absorbent pad.

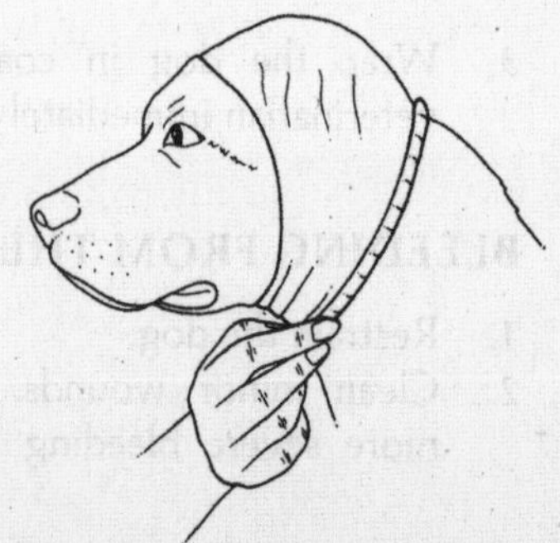

Fig. 3: Apply a tube sock bandage

Wrap gauze or torn sheets around the ear and head or pull a tube sock with the toe cut off over the dog's head to prevent the dog shaking its ear and starting bleeding once more.

3. See your veterinarian the same day.

BLEEDING NOSE

1. Restrain the dog and apply a cold pack to the nose. (Do not muzzle the dog. This interferes with breathing through the mouth.)
2. Help a clot to form by holding an absorbent pad over the nostril.
3. Nosebleeds are caused by trauma or other damage in the nose. Telephone your veterinarian for advice.

BLEEDING LIMB

1. For minor bleeding, restrain the dog, apply pressure to the bleeding wound with an absorbent pad, clean with 3% hydrogen peroxide and wrap the leg in gauze and bandage.
2. When bleeding is severe, bright red and spurting, apply very firm pressure with the thumb or finger directly over the artery. If the bleeding artery is superficial, use little or no padding. Limbs are the most frequently cut areas.

Fig. 4: Stop deep bleeding on the front leg

With your thumb on the outside, grasp the front leg halfway between the shoulder and elbow. Press firmly with the flat of your fingers to reduce bleeding.

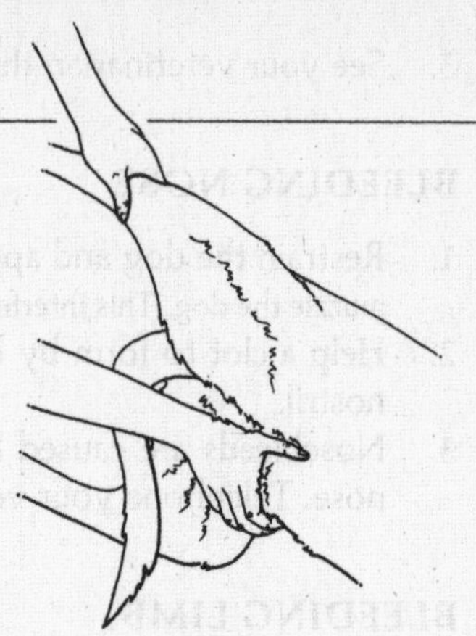

Fig. 5: Stop deep bleeding on the back leg

Press the heel of your hand firmly into the groin. Alternatively, feel for the pulse with your fingers then apply firm pressure to stop blood flowing.

3. Use a tie or piece of torn sheet as a tourniquet.
4. Elevate the leg above the heart.
5. Get veterinary attention immediately.

BLEEDING PAW

1. Restrain the dog and clean minor wounds with 3% hydrogen peroxide. Look for and remove visible foreign objects such as pieces of glass. (Do not use antiseptics that sting.)
2. Using a clean absorbent pad, apply pressure. If blood seeps through, do not remove the pad, add more padding.
3. If bleeding stops within four minutes, wrap the paw in gauze and elastic bandage. Telephone your veterinarian for advice.
4. If bleeding continues after four minutes, apply pressure to the pressure point then wrap the paw tightly and take the dog to your veterinarian immediately.

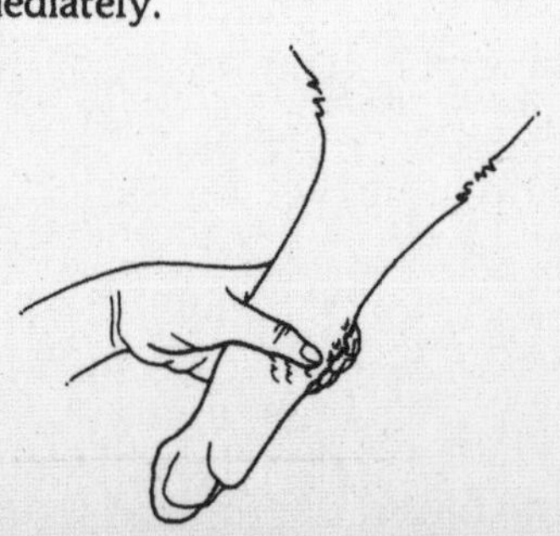

Fig. 6: Stop bleeding from paws

With your thumb at the back of the paw, grasp the leg just above the paw. Squeeze firmly.

5. Alternatively, using a tie or torn piece of soft material, apply a tourniquet and take to your veterinarian immediately. (Do not leave a tight tourniquet on the paw for more than fifteen minutes. Loosen it for two minutes then tighten again only if absolutely necessary. Used wrongly, tourniquets can be extremely damaging.)

BLEEDING NAIL

1. Restrain the dog and apply a clean absorbent pad to the bleeding nail.
2. Only remove the broken nail if it is hanging so loose that it moves easily when you touch it. Give it a quick pull with your fingers.

Fig. 7: Broken nails

(a) This nail can be removed with a quick pull.

(b) Do not try to remove this nail. Get veterinary treatment to remove pain and control infection.

3. If the nail is bleeding but still partly attached, cover with gauze and elastic bandage and see your veterinarian within twenty-four hours. (If bleeding occurs while cutting your dog's nails because you cut one too short, apply pressure with a clean absorbent pad for two minutes. Apply a ferrous sulphate or silver nitrate stick (available from pet shops). If bleeding persists, bandage the pad on to the paw with gauze and adhesive. Keep the bandage on for twenty-four hours.)

BLEEDING TAIL

1. Tails bleed profusely. Apply pressure to stop bleeding.

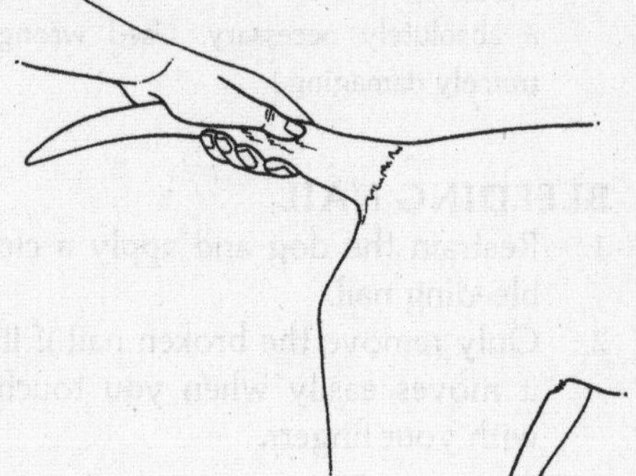

Fig. 8: The tail pressure point

With your thumb below and in the soft middle of the tail and your fingers above, apply pressure with your thumb to control bleeding.

2. Apply an absorbent pad and wrap it in place with a gauze and adhesive bandage.
3. If the tail is long enough, wrap it and bandage it to the side of the dog. (Tail wagging increases bleeding and can damage the bleeding area, interfering with repair.)
4. If the tip of the tail is bleeding, see a veterinarian within twenty-four hours. (Crushed tail tips are notoriously difficult to repair. It may be necessary to amputate back to healthy tissue that will heal normally.)

BLOAT

Bloat occurs when a dog's stomach fills with gas. The swollen, gas filled stomach expands, pressing on the diaphragm and interfering with breathing. If the stomach twists on itself, which it often does, catastrophic and often irreversible shock results. Death ensues rapidly.

Treat suspected bloat as an extreme emergency and get veterinary help as quickly as possible.

WATCH FOR SHOCK

Pale or white gums, rapid breathing, weak and rapid pulse, cold extremities, general weakness.

(For treatment of shock see under **Shock** on page 10.)

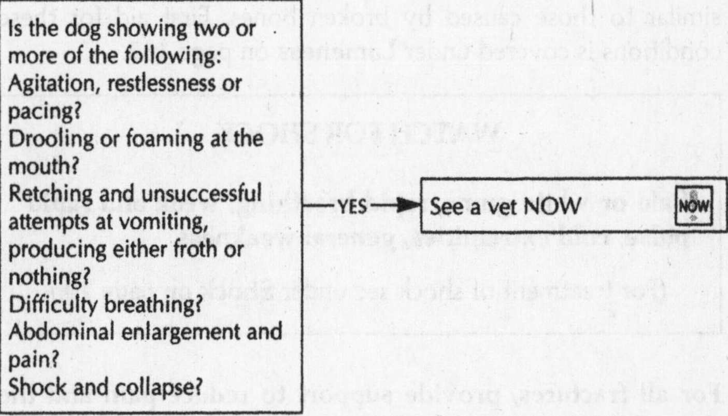
Is the dog showing two or more of the following:
Agitation, restlessness or pacing?
Drooling or foaming at the mouth?
Retching and unsuccessful attempts at vomiting, producing either froth or nothing?
Difficulty breathing?
Abdominal enlargement and pain?
Shock and collapse?
YES
See a vet NOW
NOW

(Bloat occurs most frequently in large dogs with deep chests; breeds such as Irish Setters, Great Danes and Weimaraners. It may be brought on by overeating, over drinking, exercising and especially rolling after a meal. There are other unknown genetic and environmental factors. Bloat can happen at any age.)

First aid for bloat:

1. Transport to the nearest veterinarian as quickly as possible, treating for shock during the journey.

BONES

Bones are most often damaged through injuries caused by traffic accidents and falls. If the bone breaks through the skin and is **open**, it can easily become infected. **Closed** fractures, where the bone does not break through, and dislocations, where a bone is pulled out of its socket, are just as dangerous and painful to the dog but not as readily apparent. If a fracture is closed one of your important objectives is to prevent it from becoming open.

Muscle, ligament and tendon injuries can cause clinical signs similar to those caused by broken bones. First aid for these conditions is covered under **Lameness** on page 132.

> **WATCH FOR SHOCK**
>
> **Pale or white gums, rapid breathing, weak and rapid pulse, cold extremities, general weakness.**
>
> (For treatment of shock see under **Shock** on page 10.)

For all fractures, provide support to reduce pain and the risk of further injuries during transport. Do not try to reset fractures. Do not use antiseptics or any type of ointments on open fractures.

SPINAL FRACTURES

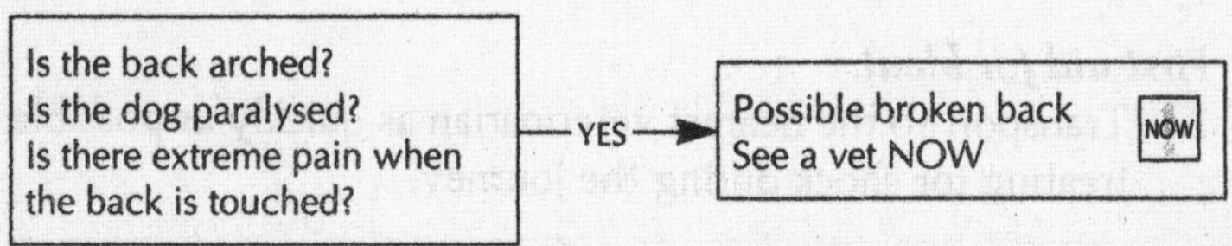
Is the back arched?
Is the dog paralysed?
Is there extreme pain when the back is touched?
YES
Possible broken back
See a vet NOW
NOW

1. Muzzle if necessary.
2. Without bending the dog's back, gently pull the dog on to a flat board and strap it down, avoiding pressure on the neck.

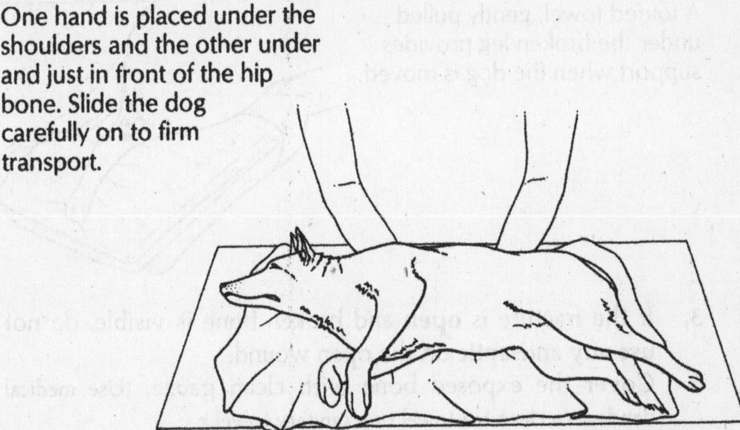

Fig. 1: Avoid manipulating the back

One hand is placed under the shoulders and the other under and just in front of the hip bone. Slide the dog carefully on to firm transport.

3. Take the dog to the veterinarian immediately. **Do not try to splint a broken back.**

LIMB FRACTURES

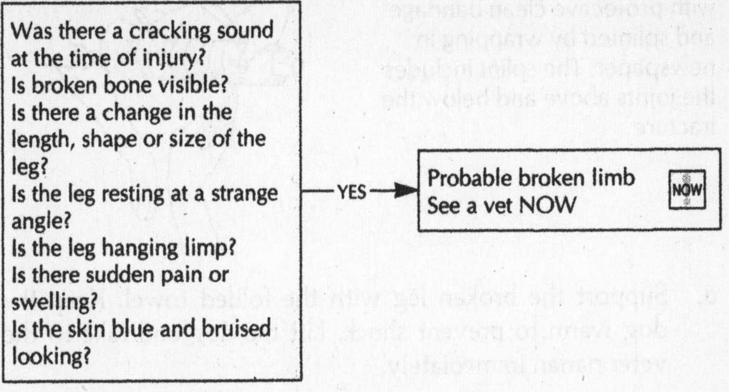
Was there a cracking sound at the time of injury?
Is broken bone visible?
Is there a change in the length, shape or size of the leg?
Is the leg resting at a strange angle?
Is the leg hanging limp?
Is there sudden pain or swelling?
Is the skin blue and bruised looking?
YES
Probable broken limb
See a vet NOW
NOW

1. Muzzle the dog if necessary.
2. Gently slide a clean towel under the limb.

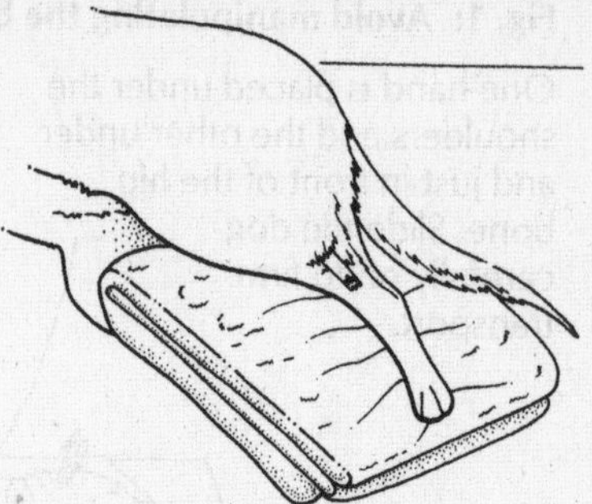

Fig. 2: Support the broken leg

A folded towel, gently pulled under the broken leg provides support when the dog is moved.

3. If the fracture is **open** and broken bone is visible, do not use any antiseptic on the open wound.
4. Cover the exposed bone with clean gauze. (Use medical bandage, a clean tea towel or a sanitary towel.)
5. If the fracture is **closed** there is no need to apply gauze. Use a roll of newspaper, a magazine or similar material to splint the leg. (If this causes severe pain, stop. Provide support only with the folded towel.)

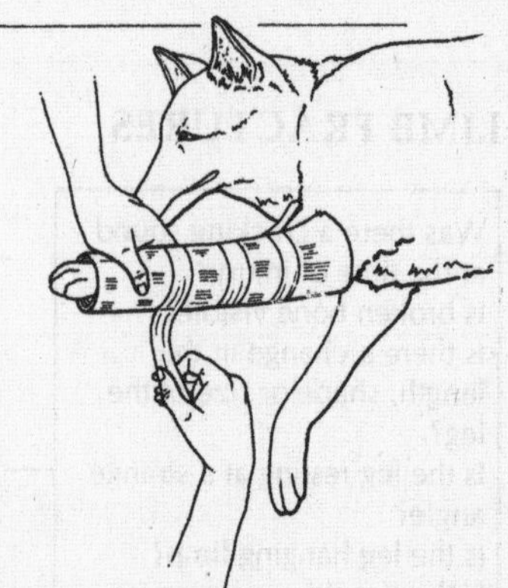

Fig. 3: The wound is protected

The exposed bone is covered with protective clean bandage and splinted by wrapping in newspaper. The splint includes the joints above and below the fracture.

6. Support the broken leg with the folded towel. Keep the dog warm to prevent shock. Lift the dog and take to the veterinarian immediately.

Do not try to reset broken bones. The splint prevents further damage to nerves, blood vessels and other tissues.

Resetting, including repositioning dislocated bones should be carried out by the veterinarian under general anaesthetic.

RIB FRACTURES

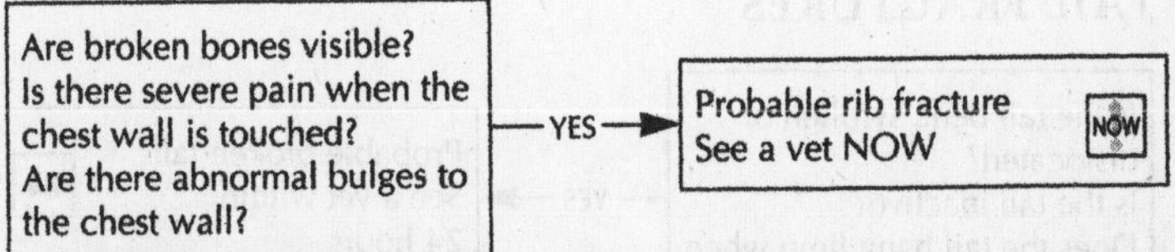
Are broken bones visible?
Is there severe pain when the chest wall is touched?
Are there abnormal bulges to the chest wall?
YES
Probable rib fracture
See a vet NOW
NOW

A sucking sound means the chest cavity has been penetrated.

1. Muzzle the dog if necessary, but only if it is having no difficulty breathing
2. If there are open wounds, cover them with clean gauze.
3. Wrap torn sheets firmly around the chest but not so firm that they interfere with breathing.

Fig. 4: Wrap the chest wall

Gauze bandage or torn sheet is wrapped around the chest wall to provide firm support. Do not bandage if there are signs of shock.

4. If part of the chest wall is softly bulging, wrap this area first, using enough pressure to eliminate the bulge. (A hard bulge is usually the broken end of a rib. A soft bulge means the

lung is possibly punctured, deep muscles are damaged and air is trying to escape.)

5. Take the dog to the veterinarian immediately. (Do not pick up or support the dog by its chest.)

TAIL FRACTURES

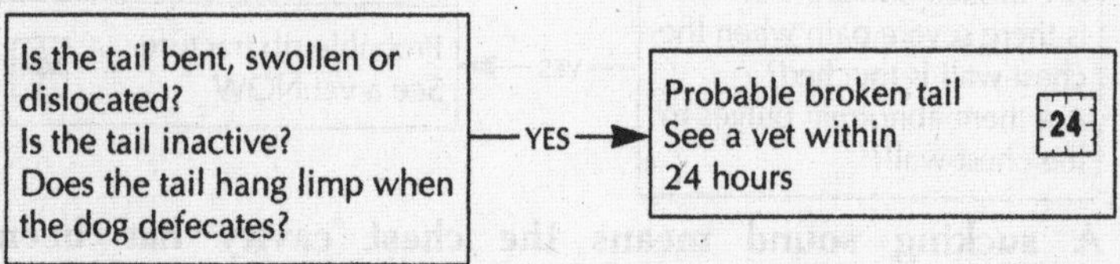
Is the tail bent, swollen or dislocated?
Is the tail inactive?
Does the tail hang limp when the dog defecates?
YES
Probable broken tail
See a vet within
24 hours
24

1. Successfully bandaging a tail is extremely difficult, even for experts. If the dog does not seem to be in pain, there is no bleeding and no bones are protruding, make an appointment to see your veterinarian during the next twenty-four hours.

BREATHING PROBLEMS

Although some breathing difficulties are minor, others can be life threatening. Remember, rapid or light breathing can mean shock.

> **WATCH FOR SHOCK**
>
> **Pale or white gums, rapid breathing, weak and rapid pulse, cold extremities, general weakness.**
>
> (For treatment of shock see under **Shock** on page 10.)

Breathing problems can originate in the air passages themselves, but they can also be secondary to serious conditions in other parts of the body. Treat most breathing difficulties as potentially serious emergencies.

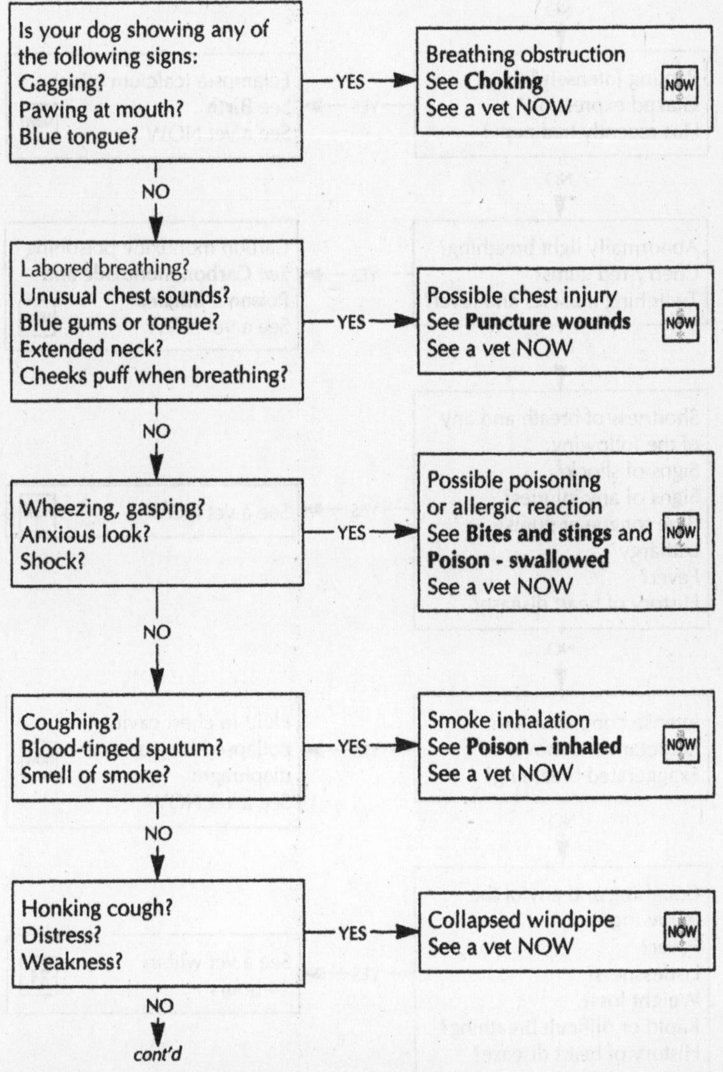
Is your dog showing any of the following signs:
Gagging?
Pawing at mouth?
Blue tongue?
YES
Breathing obstruction
See **Choking**
See a vet NOW
NOW
NO
Labored breathing?
Unusual chest sounds?
Blue gums or tongue?
Extended neck?
Cheeks puff when breathing?
YES
Possible chest injury
See **Puncture wounds**
See a vet NOW
NOW
NO
Wheezing, gasping?
Anxious look?
Shock?
YES
Possible poisoning
or allergic reaction
See **Bites and stings** and
Poison - swallowed
See a vet NOW
NOW
NO
Coughing?
Blood-tinged sputum?
Smell of smoke?
YES
Smoke inhalation
See **Poison – inhaled**
See a vet NOW
NOW
NO
Honking cough?
Distress?
Weakness?
YES
Collapsed windpipe
See a vet NOW
NOW
NO
cont'd

BRATHING PROBLEMS

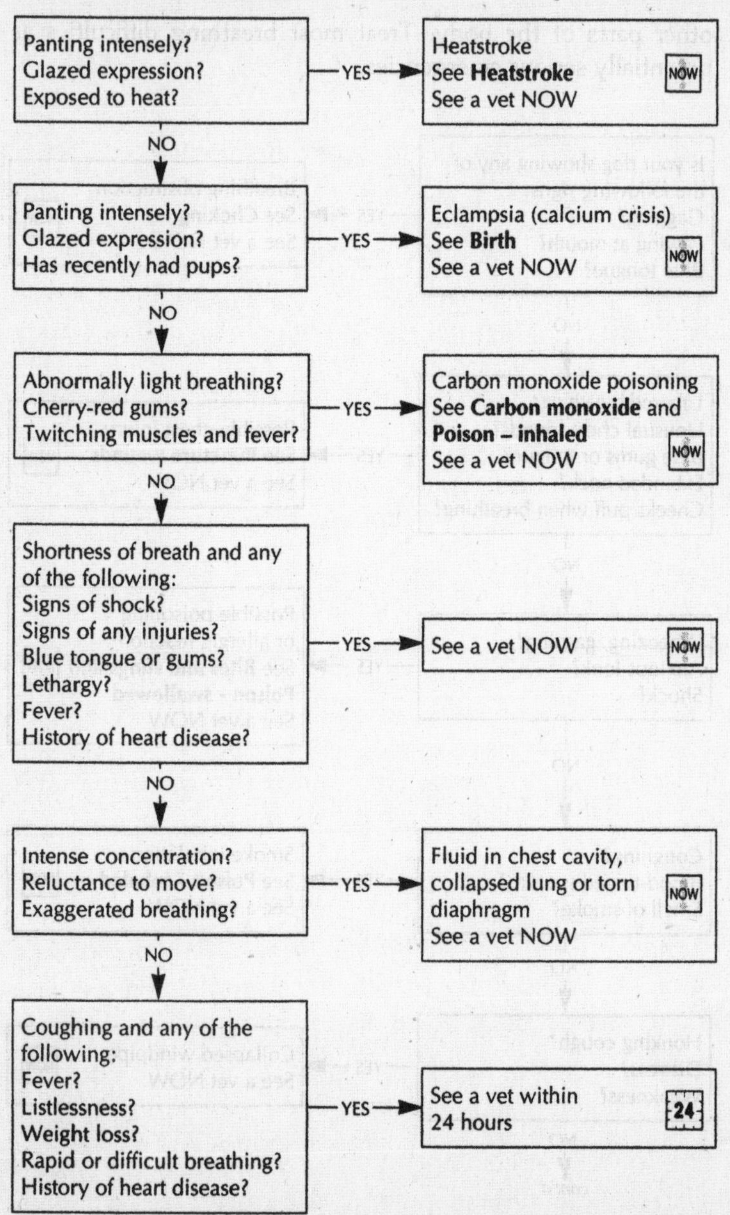
Panting intensely?
Glazed expression?
Exposed to heat?
YES
Heatstroke
See **Heatstroke**
See a vet NOW
NOW
NO
Panting intensely?
Glazed expression?
Has recently had pups?
YES
Eclampsia (calcium crisis)
See **Birth**
See a vet NOW
NOW
NO
Abnormally light breathing?
Cherry-red gums?
Twitching muscles and fever?
YES
Carbon monoxide poisoning
See **Carbon monoxide** and **Poison – inhaled**
See a vet NOW
NOW
NO
Shortness of breath and any of the following:
Signs of shock?
Signs of any injuries?
Blue tongue or gums?
Lethargy?
Fever?
History of heart disease?
YES
See a vet NOW
NOW
NO
Intense concentration?
Reluctance to move?
Exaggerated breathing?
YES
Fluid in chest cavity, collapsed lung or torn diaphragm
See a vet NOW
NOW
NO
Coughing and any of the following:
Fever?
Listlessness?
Weight loss?
Rapid or difficult breathing?
History of heart disease?
YES
See a vet within 24 hours
24

ARTIFICIAL RESPIRATION

If your dog has stopped breathing:

1. Place the dog on its side. Clear the airway of debris and pull the tongue forward.

Fig. 1: Clear the airway

Any material blocking the throat or nose is removed.

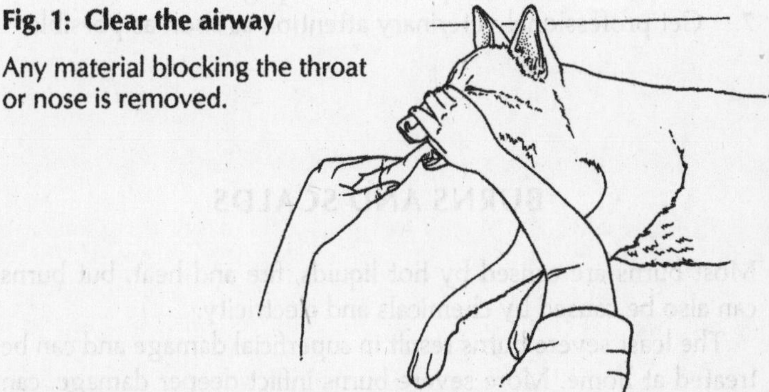

2. Close the dog's mouth. With your hand around the muzzle, place your mouth over the dog's nose and blow in until you see the chest expand.

Fig. 2: Breathe into the dog's lungs

Your hand on the muzzle creates an airtight seal.

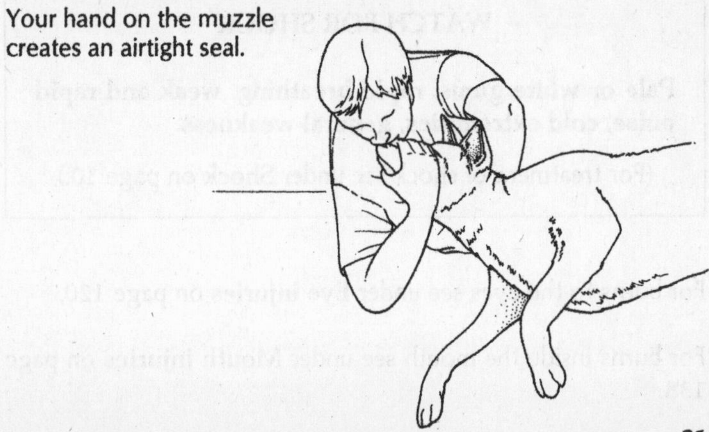

3. Take your mouth away and let the lungs deflate.
4. Repeat this procedure ten to twenty times per minute.
5. Check the pulse every ten seconds to ensure the heart is still beating.
6. If the heart is not beating, give heart massage in conjunction with artificial respiration. (See page 14.)
7. Get professional veterinary attention as soon as possible.

BURNS AND SCALDS

Most burns are caused by hot liquids, fire and heat, but burns can also be caused by chemicals and electricity.

The least severe burns result in superficial damage and can be treated at home. More severe burns inflict deeper damage, can lead to shock, sometimes even days later, and need immediate veterinary treatment.

Do not underestimate the seriousness of burns. It is sometimes the case that burns to even relatively small areas of the body can be life threatening.

WATCH FOR SHOCK

Pale or white gums, rapid breathing, weak and rapid pulse, cold extremities, general weakness.

(For treatment of shock see under **Shock** on page 10.)

For burns to the eyes see under **Eye injuries** on page 120.

For burns inside the mouth see under **Mouth injuries** on page 138.

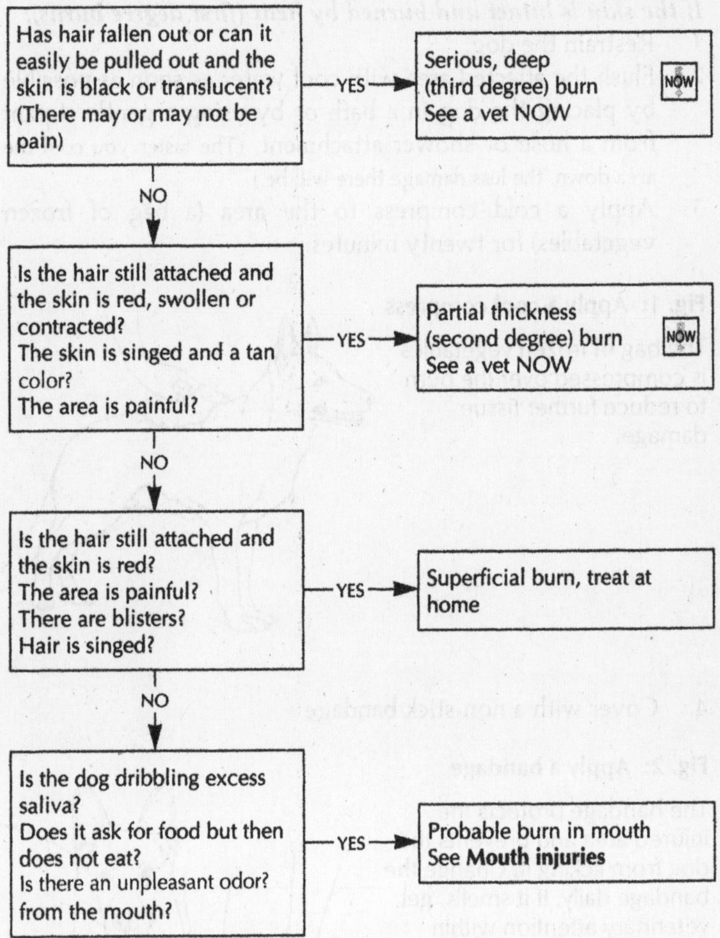
Has hair fallen out or can it easily be pulled out and the skin is black or translucent? (There may or may not be pain)
YES
Serious, deep (third degree) burn See a vet NOW
NOW
NO
Is the hair still attached and the skin is red, swollen or contracted? The skin is singed and a tan color? The area is painful?
YES
Partial thickness (second degree) burn See a vet NOW
NOW
NO
Is the hair still attached and the skin is red? The area is painful? There are blisters? Hair is singed?
YES
Superficial burn, treat at home
NO
Is the dog dribbling excess saliva? Does it ask for food but then does not eat? Is there an unpleasant odor? from the mouth?
YES
Probable burn in mouth See Mouth injuries

Do not apply ointments, creams, butter or margarine to burns. They do not help.

If a burn has been caused by chemicals, wear rubber gloves so that your hands are not burned.

If a burn has been caused by biting an electric cord, make sure the electric supply is cut off before touching the cord or the dog.

If the skin is intact and burned by heat (first degree burns):

1. Restrain the dog.
2. Flush the affected area with cool water as soon as possible by placing the dog in a bath or by using a gentle stream from a hose or shower attachment. (The faster you cool the area down, the less damage there will be.)
3. Apply a cold compress to the area (a bag of frozen vegetables) for twenty minutes.

Fig. 1: Apply a cool compress

The bag of frozen vegetables is compressed over the burn to reduce further tissue damage.

4. Cover with a non-stick bandage.

Fig. 2: Apply a bandage

The bandage protects the injured area and prevents the dog from licking it. Change the bandage daily. If it smells, get veterinary attention within twenty-four hours.

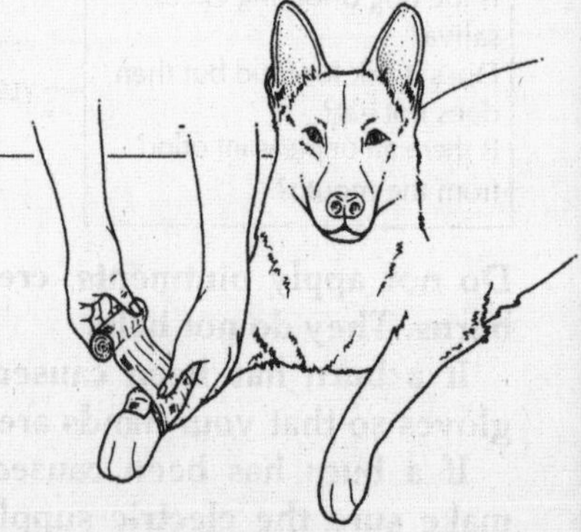

5. Telephone your veterinarian for further advice.

If the skin is intact and burned by chemicals:

1. Remove any contaminated collars, clothing or harnesses.
2. Continue flushing the area for twenty minutes, making sure that the chemical washed off does not burn any other part of the dog's body. Use mild detergent or shampoo. In the case of known acid burns, rinse with baking soda (one teaspoon per pint of water). If the inside of the mouth is burned, place the dog on its side and pour repeated cups of cool water through the mouth. Alternatively, flush the mouth using a garden hose.
3. Cover superficial chemical burns with a non-sticking bandage.
4. Telephone your veterinarian for further advice.

If the skin is burned partly or totally through (second and third degree burns):

1. Look for signs of shock and treat if necessary.
2. Apply a clean, dry dressing to the burns. Avoid using cotton or other loose-fibred materials that stick to wounds.
3. Wrap torn sheeting or other soft material around the burned area.
4. Take the dog immediately to a veterinarian.

- Reduce the risks of scalds and burns:
- Do not let your dog lie in the kitchen where hot liquids might accidentally spill on it.
- Do not pass hot foods over your dog's head, and do not let your dog near the barbecue when it is hot.
- Keep your dog away when you use dangerous chemicals such as oven, toilet or drain cleaners.
- Do not leave a pup between two and eight months old alone in a room without making sure that all electrical appliances have been unplugged.

CARBON MONOXIDE

Carbon monoxide poisoning may occur if propane gas heaters and cookers or indoor barbecues leak in unventilated places. Older cars without catalytic converters also emit carbon monoxide. When camping, never leave your dog in the tent with the propane heater on.

Do not put yourself in danger by trying to rescue a dog. Make sure you have fresh air to breathe.

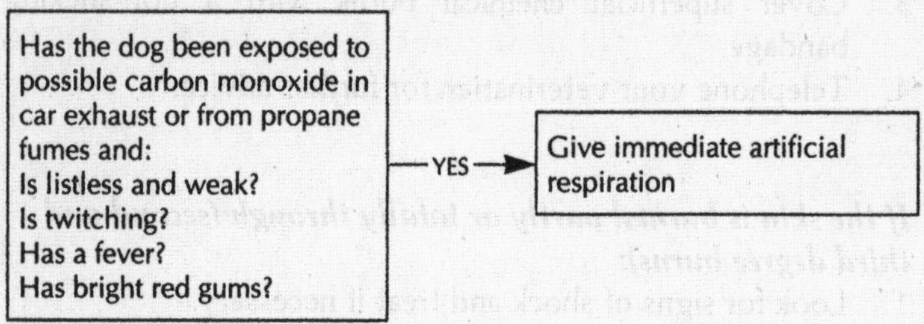
Has the dog been exposed to possible carbon monoxide in car exhaust or from propane fumes and:
Is listless and weak?
Is twitching?
Has a fever?
Has bright red gums?
YES
Give immediate artificial respiration

If the dog has stopped breathing:

1. Remove it from further danger.
2. Give artificial respiration if breathing has stopped.
3. Give CPR if breathing and the heart have both stopped.
4. If breathing resumes, contact your veterinarian for further advice.
5. When possible, continue CPR on the way to getting immediate veterinary attention.

CHOKING

Dogs readily put almost anything in their mouths. Objects sometimes get stuck on teeth or flat against the hard palate, causing the dog to paw at its mouth. If an object blocks the windpipe, choking follows. Common causes of choking are hard rubber balls, gristle and moisture-swollen chewsticks. If your dog is choking, do not wait for veterinary help, your dog risks suffocating to death.

For foreign bodies stuck in the mouth not causing choking see **Mouth injuries** on page 135.

Choking is frightening. An otherwise calm dog is liable to bite. Take extra care to avoid getting injured.

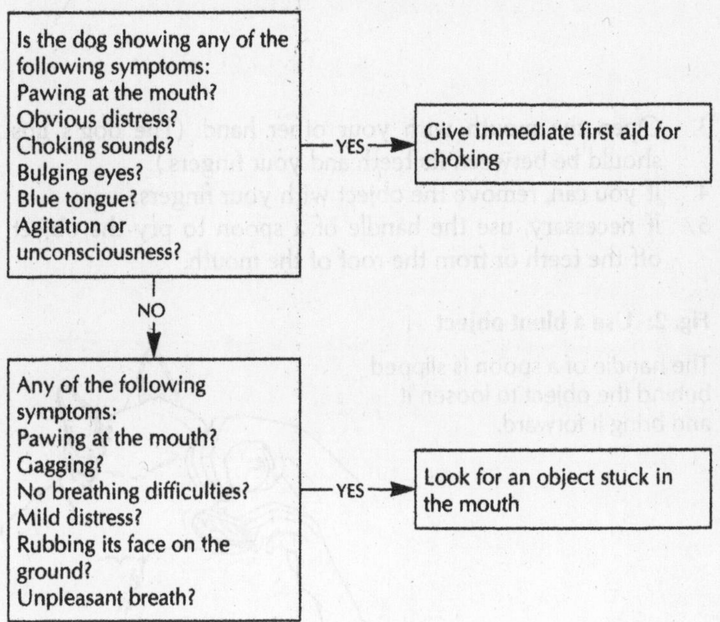
Is the dog showing any of the following symptoms:
Pawing at the mouth?
Obvious distress?
Choking sounds?
Bulging eyes?
Blue tongue?
Agitation or unconsciousness?
YES
Give immediate first aid for choking
NO
Any of the following symptoms:
Pawing at the mouth?
Gagging?
No breathing difficulties?
Mild distress?
Rubbing its face on the ground?
Unpleasant breath?
YES
Look for an object stuck in the mouth

If the dog is conscious:

1. Restrain the dog but do not muzzle it.
2. Open the mouth by grasping the upper jaw with one hand and pressing the lips over the upper teeth.

Fig. 1: The mouth is opened

The thumb presses on one side and the fingers on the other so the upper lips cover the teeth.

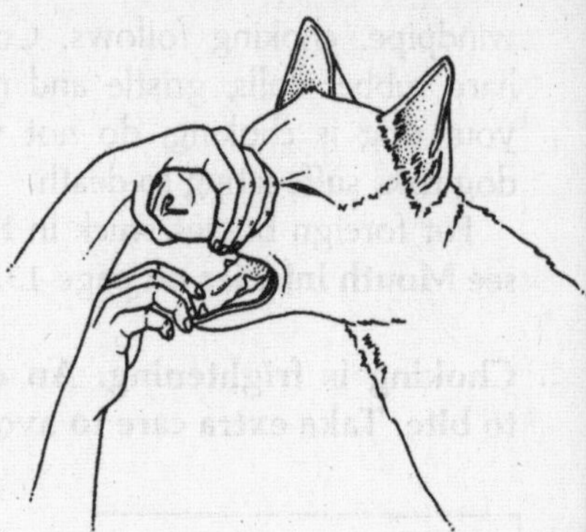

3. Open the mouth with your other hand. (The dog's lips should be between its teeth and your fingers.)
4. If you can, remove the object with your fingers.
5. If necessary, use the handle of a spoon to pry the object off the teeth or from the roof of the mouth.

Fig. 2: Use a blunt object

The handle of a spoon is slipped behind the object to loosen it and bring it forward.

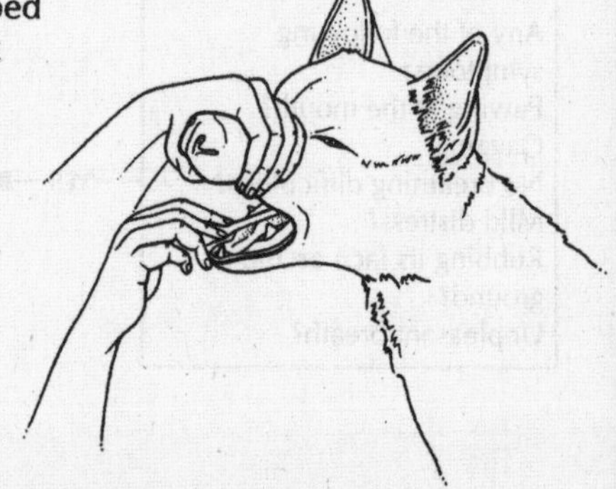

Large dog

1. If the dog is standing, stand over it, put your arms around its belly, make a fist and squeeze firmly up and forward just behind the rib cage. (This is identical to the Heimlich manuever.)

Fig. 3: The hands are positioned

As you would when a person chokes, squeeze sharply just below the rib cage.

If the dog is unconscious or is still choking and you cannot see the object:

Small dog

1. Hold the dog by its thighs and gently shake and swing it.

Fig. 4: Shake the dog

The thighs are held firmly. Swinging allows gravity to assist. If this is not successful after one minute, apply abdominal pressure.

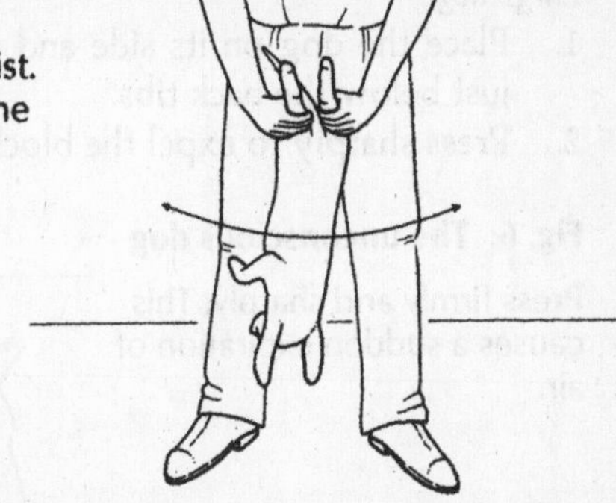

2. Place the dog on its side.
3. Using one hand to support the back, grab the abdomen

just behind the ribs and squeeze upwards and forwards towards the throat. (This is a variation of the Heimlich maneuver you would use on a person choking.)

Fig. 5: Pressure expels air from the lungs

A sharp squeeze produces pressure in the windpipe. This helps dislodge the blockage.

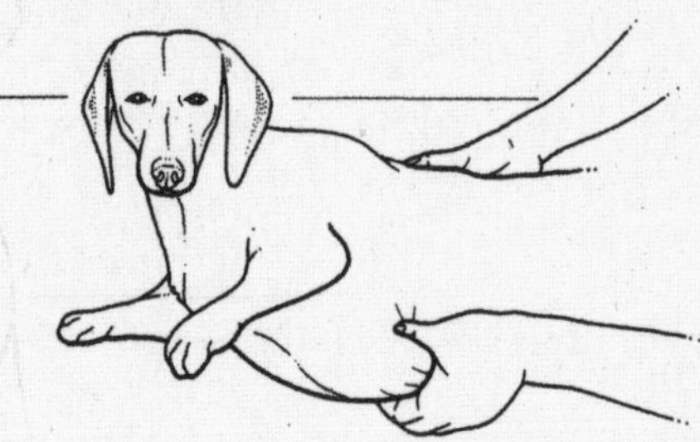

4. Sweep your fingers through the mouth and remove the dislodged object. You may have to probe deeply in the back of the throat, making a 'hook' with your index finger.
5. Give artificial respiration or CPR as necessary.
6. If artificial respiration or CPR is necessary, get immediate veterinary assistance.

Large dog

1. Place the dog on its side and put the heels of both hands just below the back ribs.
2. Press sharply to expel the blockage.

Fig. 6: The unconscious dog

Press firmly and sharply. This causes a sudden expiration of air.

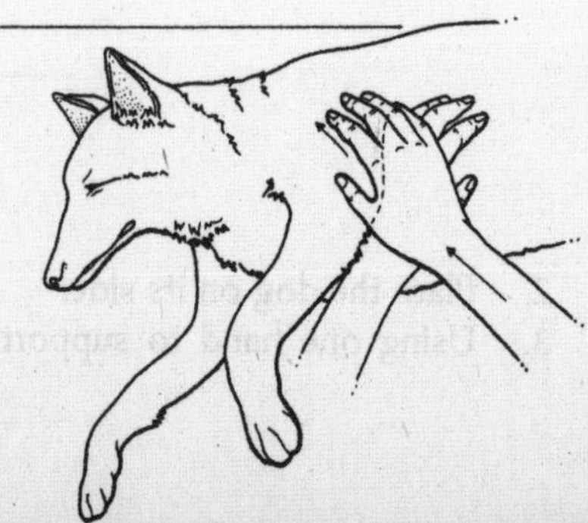

3. Sweep your fingers through the dog's mouth looking for the expelled item. You may have to probe deeply in the back of the throat, making a 'hook' with your index finger.
4. Repeat until you are successful.
5. When the air passage has been cleared, give artificial respiration or CPR as necessary.
6. See your veterinarian. The object might have injured the dog's throat and further swelling might occur.

Do not try to swing a large dog. It is difficult to work up sufficient momentum and you are likely to cause further injuries.

COMA

When a dog appears to be asleep but has no pain response it is in a coma. Comas are most common in diabetic dogs but also can be caused by extremes of temperature, certain drugs and poisons, overwhelming infections and shock.

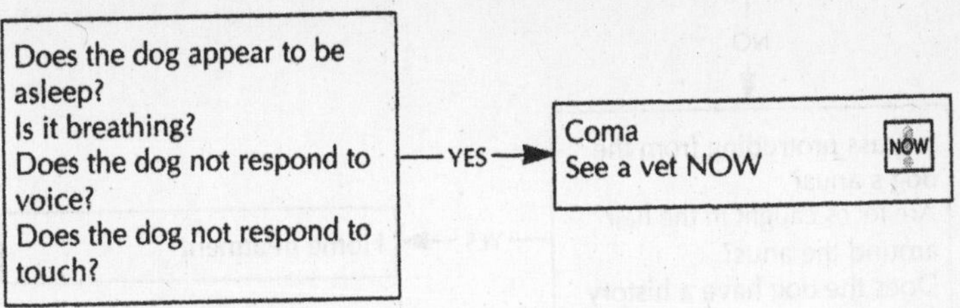
Does the dog appear to be asleep?
Is it breathing?
Does the dog not respond to voice?
Does the dog not respond to touch?
YES
Coma
See a vet NOW
NOW

1. Make sure the airway is not blocked.
2. Eliminate or treat the specific cause of the coma if this is known.
3. Monitor breathing and heart.
4. Provide artificial respiration or CPR if necessary.
5. Seek veterinary help immediately.

CONSTIPATION

The most common cause of constipation is an indigestible object like a piece of bone that is too large or dry to pass easily through the anus. Constipation is also caused by slower intestinal movements, hernias, enlarged prostates in male dogs or hair or grass that has been swallowed. Severe diarrhea causes straining that can be mistaken for constipation.

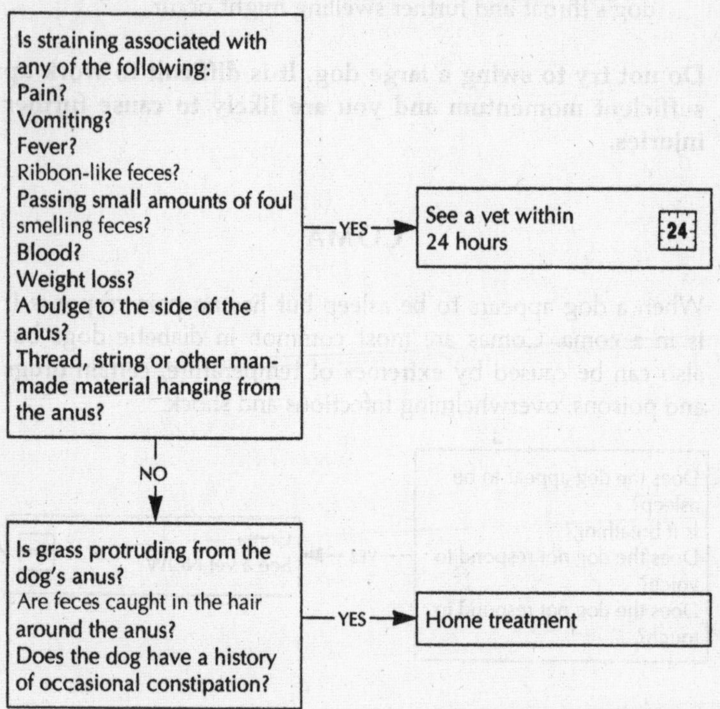
Is straining associated with any of the following:
Pain?
Vomiting?
Fever?
Ribbon-like feces?
Passing small amounts of foul smelling feces?
Blood?
Weight loss?
A bulge to the side of the anus?
Thread, string or other man-made material hanging from the anus?
YES
See a vet within 24 hours
24
NO
Is grass protruding from the dog's anus?
Are feces caught in the hair around the anus?
Does the dog have a history of occasional constipation?
YES
Home treatment

1. If grass is visible at the anal opening, put on a rubber glove and gently ease it out. **Do not attempt to pull out string or thread**, you may cause serious internal damage. (Control your dog's habit of eating grass.)

2. If feces are stuck in the hair around the anus, trim the hair and matted feces away with scissors. Wash the inflamed anal region with warm soapy water and apply soothing water-soluble (K-Y) jelly. (Sometimes it is necessary to soak the dog's bottom in warm water prior to trimming, as some dogs, especially small ones with long hair such as Yorkshire Terriers, Lhasa Apsos and Shih Tzus, become frantic with discomfort. Soaking softens the feces stuck to the hair and skin.)
3. If there is a history of intermittent constipation, add mineral oil to the dog's food at a dose rate of 1 teaspoon per 5 Kg (11 lbs) body weight. (Do not give mineral oil directly by mouth. If it gets in the lungs, which it can easily do, it may cause pneumonia.)
4. Take your dog's temperature. If it is elevated, if there is blood on the thermometer or the thermometer hits a hard blockage, take your dog to your veterinarian within twenty-four hours. Your dog may be hospitalized and given enemas to relieve the constipation.

Constipation is more common in older than younger dogs. Use purpose made laxatives when necessary to keep stools softer. Make sure your dog has adequate water to drink. Do not give your dog bones, provide a nylon chew toy.

CONVULSIONS AND SEIZURES

Convulsions or seizures cause a dog to appear to lose control of its body. If seizures recur, the condition is usually called epilepsy. Although there are many known causes of convulsions, such as low blood sugar, liver disease, low blood calcium, poor circulation, viral and bacterial infections, poisons, scar tissue on the brain and brain tumors, in many instances it is very difficult to determine the exact cause.

CONVULSIONS AND SEIZURES

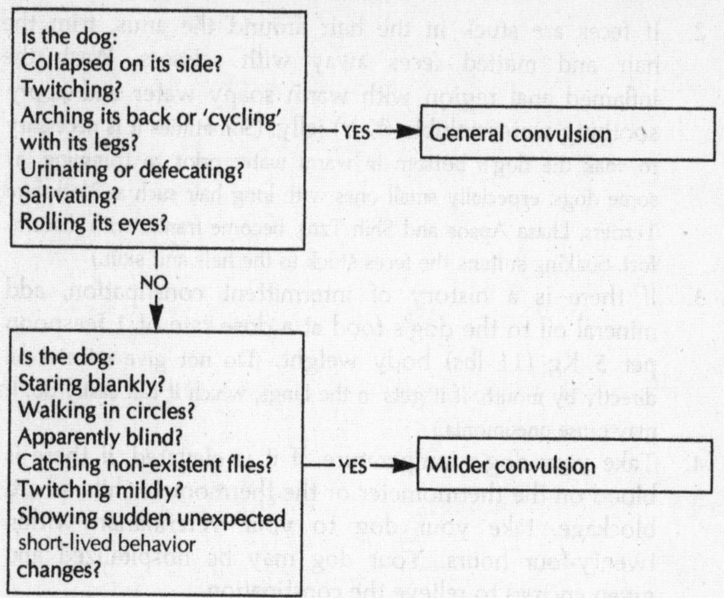
Is the dog:
Collapsed on its side?
Twitching?
Arching its back or 'cycling' with its legs?
Urinating or defecating?
Salivating?
Rolling its eyes?
YES
General convulsion
NO
Is the dog:
Staring blankly?
Walking in circles?
Apparently blind?
Catching non-existent flies?
Twitching mildly?
Showing sudden unexpected short-lived behavior changes?
YES
Milder convulsion

If a dog has a seizure, do not panic. Most convulsions are not life threatening. Avoid the dog only if you are in an area where rabies exists and you do not know the vaccination status of the dog.

1. Dogs rarely choke on their tongues. Avoid putting your fingers near the dog's mouth unless absolutely necessary. (Breeds with flat faces like Pugs and Boston Terriers can choke on their tongues, so must be observed closely. If the dog becomes unconscious, pull the tongue far out and give artificial respiration if necessary.)
2. If your dog is having a mild convulsion, gain its attention. This might prevent a full seizure from developing.
3. If a full seizure has developed get a blanket or cushions. Pull the dog away from articles on which it may injure itself and, if the seizure lasts more than a minute, wrap the dog in the blanket or surround it with cushions to protect

it from self-inflicted injuries. Unwrap the dog afterwards. Leaving it wrapped can lead to hyperthermia.

Fig. 1: Protect the dog

Cushions surround the dog to prevent rolling and protect it from hard surfaces.

4. If the seizure stops within four minutes, reduce sound and light and speak soothingly and reassuringly to the dog. Keep other dogs away.
5. If the seizure continues longer than four minutes, take the dog immediately to the veterinarian. Do not wrap the dog tightly in a blanket during the journey, this may lead to hyperthermia.
6. Keep a record of the time the seizure occurred and what the dog was doing before it happened. This helps the diagnosis if further seizures occur.

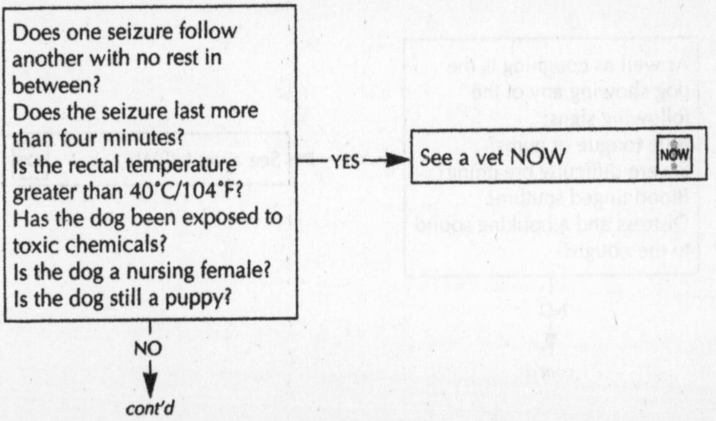
Does one seizure follow another with no rest in between?
Does the seizure last more than four minutes?
Is the rectal temperature greater than 40°C/104°F?
Has the dog been exposed to toxic chemicals?
Is the dog a nursing female?
Is the dog still a puppy?
YES
See a vet NOW
NOW
NO
cont'd

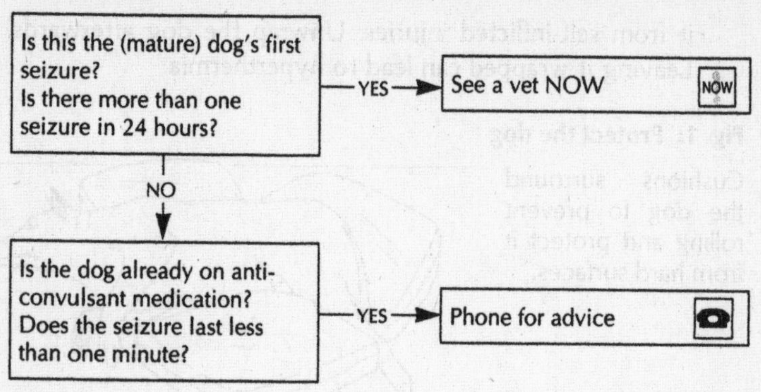
Is this the (mature) dog's first seizure?
Is there more than one seizure in 24 hours?
YES
See a vet NOW
NOW
NO
Is the dog already on anti-convulsant medication?
Does the seizure last less than one minute?
YES
Phone for advice

COUGHING

Coughing is a defence mechanism to remove unwanted material from the air passages. Coughing can be caused by allergy and pollution, but also by infections, worms, heart problems, chest disease, tumours, even a collapsed windpipe. Some causes of coughing can be treated at home. Others require veterinary attention.

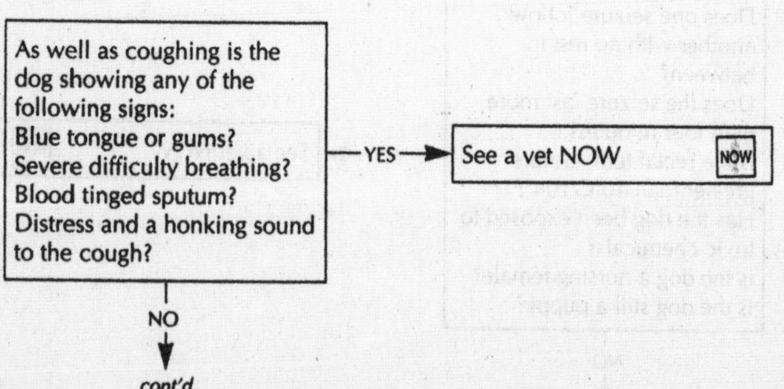
As well as coughing is the dog showing any of the following signs:
Blue tongue or gums?
Severe difficulty breathing?
Blood tinged sputum?
Distress and a honking sound to the cough?
YES
See a vet NOW
NOW
NO
cont'd

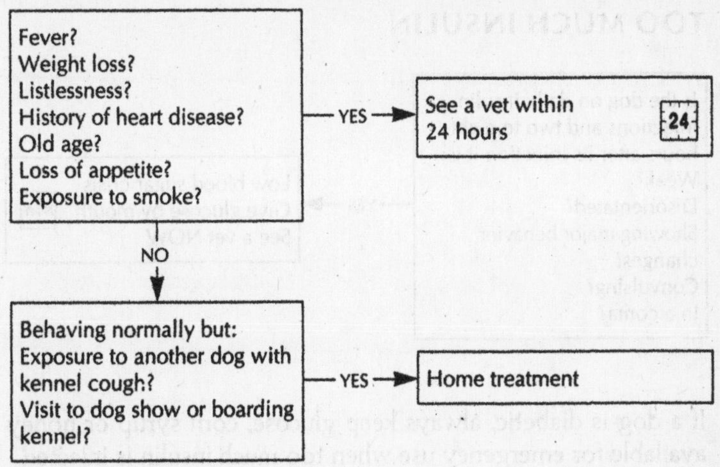
Fever?
Weight loss?
Listlessness?
History of heart disease?
Old age?
Loss of appetite?
Exposure to smoke?
YES
See a vet within 24 hours
24
NO
Behaving normally but:
Exposure to another dog with kennel cough?
Visit to dog show or boarding kennel?
YES
Home treatment

Home treatment of minor coughs:

1. Give the dog proprietary cough syrup containing an expectorant. (Do not give a cough syrup that suppresses coughing.)
2. Turn on the hot shower in the bathroom and fill the room with steam. If it is not distressed by your doing so, leave the dog in the steam filled room for up to fifteen minutes.
3. If the cough is not improving by the third day or if the dog appears unwell in any other way, get veterinary advice.

DIABETIC EMERGENCIES

Emergencies can occur when either too much or too little insulin is injected into a diabetic dog. Both are major emergencies. If untreated they can lead to coma and rapid death.

TOO MUCH INSULIN

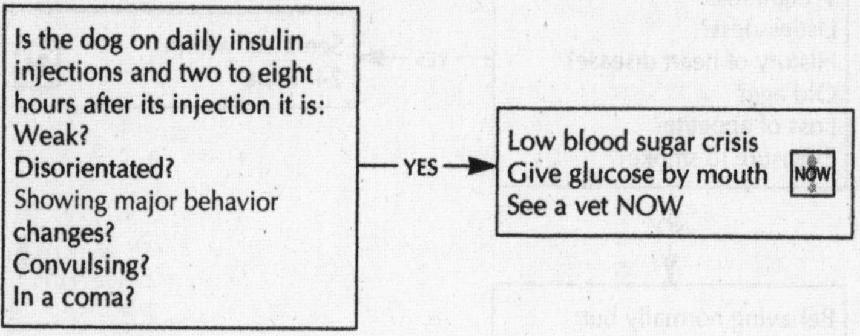
Is the dog on daily insulin injections and two to eight hours after its injection it is:
Weak?
Disorientated?
Showing major behavior changes?
Convulsing?
In a coma?
YES
Low blood sugar crisis
Give glucose by mouth
See a vet NOW
NOW

If a dog is diabetic, always keep glucose, corn syrup or honey available for emergency use when too much insulin is injected.

1. At the first sign of an insulin overdose and depressed blood sugar, syringe liquid glucose into the dog's mouth.
2. If the dog is convulsing, lift the lips and rub glucose syrup on the gums.
3. Because this may be only the beginning of the low sugar crisis, get immediate veterinary help. (Your veterinarian may give glucose intravenously.)

NOT ENOUGH INSULIN

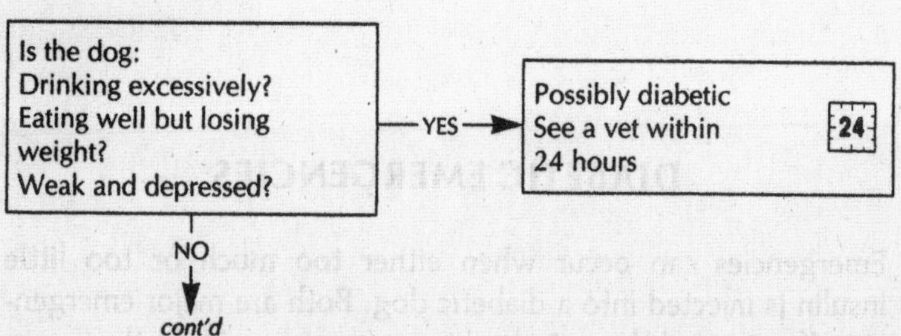
Is the dog:
Drinking excessively?
Eating well but losing weight?
Weak and depressed?
YES
Possibly diabetic
See a vet within 24 hours
24
NO
cont'd

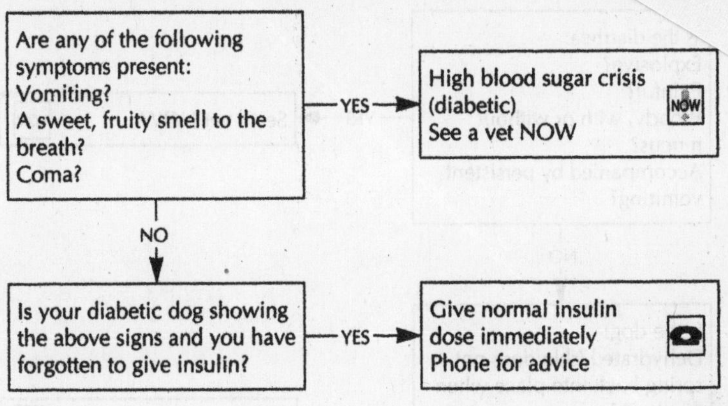
Are any of the following symptoms present:
Vomiting?
A sweet, fruity smell to the breath?
Coma?
YES
High blood sugar crisis (diabetic)
See a vet NOW
NOW
NO
Is your diabetic dog showing the above signs and you have forgotten to give insulin?
YES
Give normal insulin dose immediately
Phone for advice

DIARRHEA

Because dogs willingly taste many items, diarrhea is a common condition.

Although diarrhea is often caused by diet changes, scavenging and allergy, more serious causes such as viral infections, malabsorption conditions, tumors and metabolic failures all cause severe or persistent loose stools.

Diarrhoea with no vomiting:

1. Remove all food. Allow the dog plenty of drinking water to prevent dehydration.
2. Give kaolin mixture, one teaspoon per 5 Kg (11 lbs) every six hours.
3. If diarrhea persists for more than twenty-four hours or if blood appears, telephone your veterinarian.
4. After a twelve-hour fast, give the dog a small quantity of cooked rice and chicken. Continue with this diet until stools return to normal.

or tunafish, rinsed off

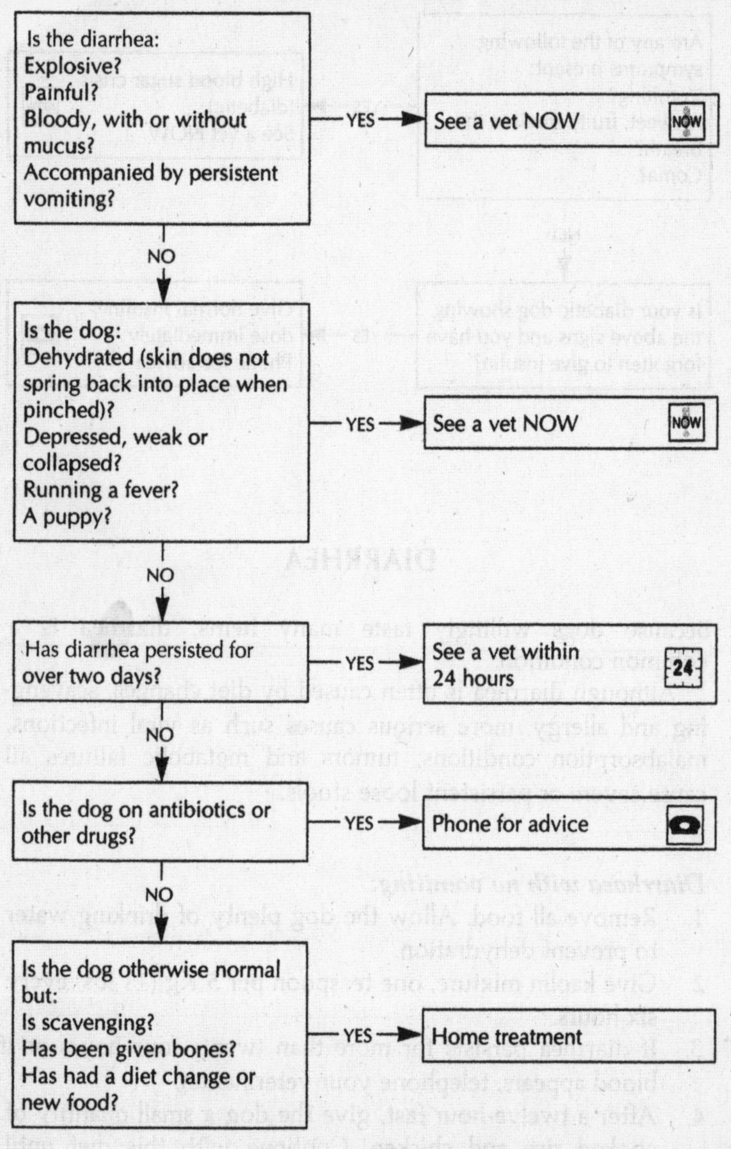
Is the diarrhea:
Explosive?
Painful?
Bloody, with or without mucus?
Accompanied by persistent vomiting?
YES
See a vet NOW
NOW
NO
Is the dog:
Dehydrated (skin does not spring back into place when pinched)?
Depressed, weak or collapsed?
Running a fever?
A puppy?
YES
See a vet NOW
NOW
NO
Has diarrhea persisted for over two days?
YES
See a vet within 24 hours
24
NO
Is the dog on antibiotics or other drugs?
YES
Phone for advice
NO
Is the dog otherwise normal but:
Is scavenging?
Has been given bones?
Has had a diet change or new food?
YES
Home treatment

Diarrhea with mild vomiting:

1. Remove all food and water for twelve hours.
2. Give the dog ice cubes to lick or small quantities of soda water every hour. (One teaspoonful for small dogs, a tablespoonful for large dogs.)
3. When vomiting has stopped, feed the dog a small quantity of cooked chicken and rice and reintroduce small quantities of water. If there is no further vomiting, feed a little more food two hours later and give kaolin mixture to coat the stomach.
4. Continue this treatment until well formed stools are passed then revert to the normal diet.

Reduce the risk of diarrhea by not giving a dog bones or small objects to play with, by not abruptly changing its diet, by not giving table scraps and by not letting the dog scavenge.

DROWNING

Near-drowning emergencies occur most frequently when dogs fall into swimming pools or canals or through ice and cannot get out. Although dogs are naturally strong swimmers, exhaustion or panic may also occur while swimming in ponds, lakes or rivers, especially if the dog is caught in a fast current. Do not put your life at risk trying to save a dog, especially from stormy seas.

1. Rescue the dog with a hooked pole through its collar when possible. Alternatively, approach the dog by boat. You should enter the water only as a last resort. If you do enter the water, take something with you that the dog can cling to.
2. If the dog is conscious, return it to land and keep it warm.
3. If the dog is unconscious, drain the lungs of water by

holding it upside down for ten to twenty seconds, giving several downward shakes.

Fig. 1: Draining a small dog's lungs

Hold the dog just above its knees and shake out water from the air passages and lungs, by swinging it from side to side and lifting up and down.

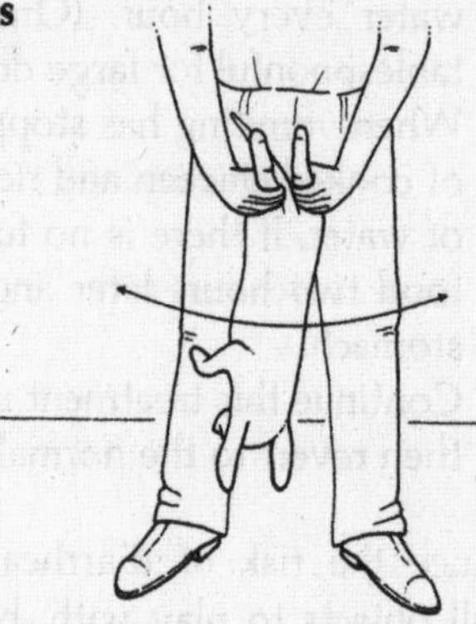

Fig. 2: Draining a large dog's lungs

The dog is lifted around its middle. Squeeze the chest firmly to help expel water.

4. Position the dog on its side with its head lower than its lungs. Clear debris from the mouth and pull out the tongue.
5. Check for a heartbeat. If there is none, begin CPR.
6. If the heart is beating but the dog is not breathing, give artificial respiration.

Serious life threatening problems can occur hours after a near-drowning incident. Take the dog for immediate veterinary attention.

WATCH FOR SHOCK

Pale or white gums, rapid breathing, weak and rapid pulse, cold extremities, general weakness.

(For treatment of shock see under Shock on page 10.)

EAR INJURIES

Sudden, violent head shaking is usually caused by a foreign object in the ear. Head shaking itself can rupture a blood vessel in the ear causing the flap to swell like a balloon and fill with blood.

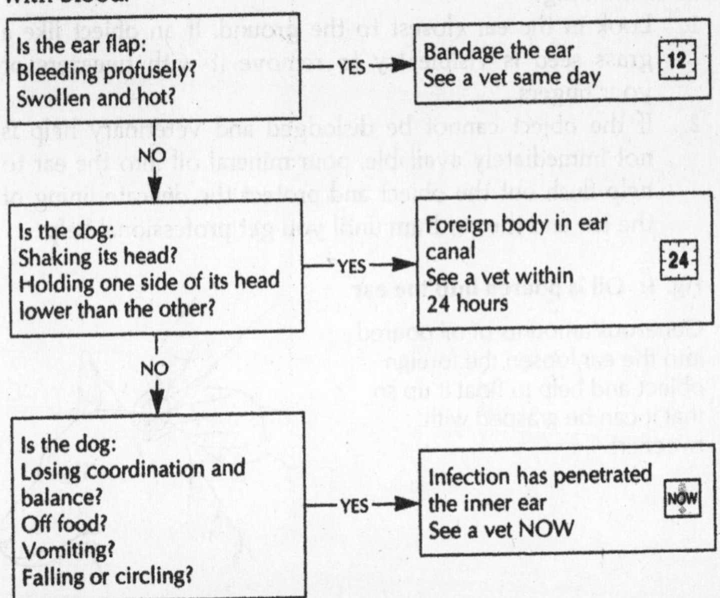
Is the ear flap:
Bleeding profusely?
Swollen and hot?
YES
Bandage the ear
See a vet same day
12
NO
Is the dog:
Shaking its head?
Holding one side of its head lower than the other?
YES
Foreign body in ear canal
See a vet within 24 hours
24
NO
Is the dog:
Losing coordination and balance?
Off food?
Vomiting?
Falling or circling?
YES
Infection has penetrated the inner ear
See a vet NOW
NOW

Bleeding ear:

1. Apply pressure with absorbent pads on both sides of the ear flap for several minutes.
2. Do not remove the pads. Place the ear back against the head and bandage using a tube sock with the toe cut out or with gauze.
3. See your veterinarian the same day.

Swollen ear:

1. Prevent further head shaking and ear flapping by bandaging the affected ear using a tube sock with the toe cut out.
2. Correct the underlying cause of head shaking by seeing your veterinarian in the next twenty-four hours to eliminate mites, foreign bodies, infection or allergy. (Swelling can be caused by abscess formation after a fight. This also requires veterinary attention.)

Head shaking:

1. Look in the ear closest to the ground. If an object like a grass seed is visible try to remove it with tweezers or your fingers.
2. If the object cannot be dislodged and veterinary help is not immediately available, pour mineral oil into the ear to help flush out the object and protect the delicate lining of the ear and the eardrum until you get professional help.

Fig. 1: Oil is poured into the ear

Generous amounts of oil poured into the ear loosen the foreign object and help to float it up so that it can be grasped with tweezers.

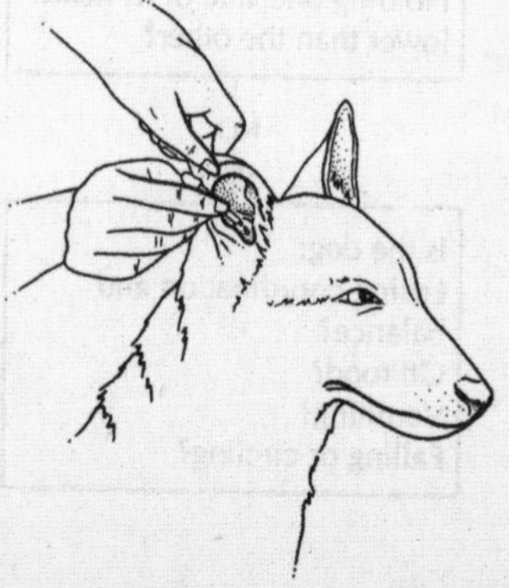

3. If you cannot get the foreign body out, bandage the ear to the head to prevent further damage until you can get veterinary assistance.

Loss of balance:

1. Prevent the dog from injuring itself by keeping it restricted to one room.
2. See your veterinarian the same day.

ELECTRIC SHOCK

Electric shock can cause cardiac arrest. It also burns the affected part of the body. Although chewing on electric cords is the most common cause of electrocution, contacts with power lines and lightning also causes usually fatal accidents. Although instances are uncommon, male dogs can receive a serious electric shock if they urinate on to exposed electric wires or unprotected electric sockets.

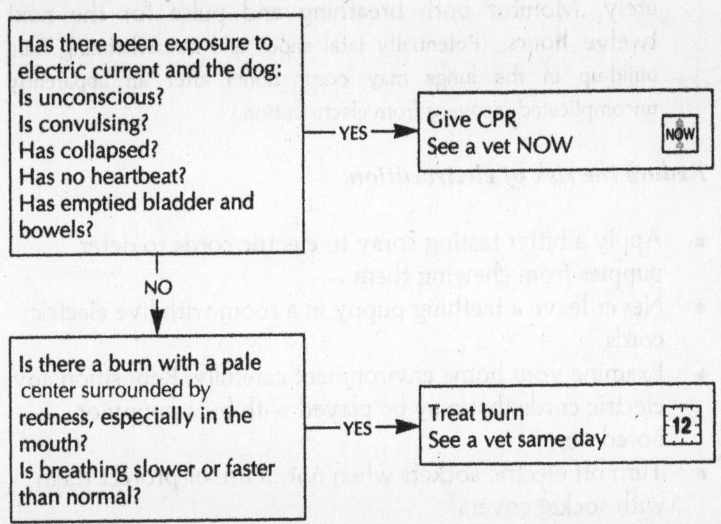
Has there been exposure to electric current and the dog:
Is unconscious?
Is convulsing?
Has collapsed?
Has no heartbeat?
Has emptied bladder and bowels?
YES
Give CPR
See a vet NOW
NOW
NO
Is there a burn with a pale center surrounded by redness, especially in the mouth?
Is breathing slower or faster than normal?
YES
Treat burn
See a vet same day
12

WATCH FOR SHOCK

Pale or white gums, rapid breathing, weak and rapid pulse, cold extremities, general weakness.

(For treatment of shock see under **Shock** on page 10.)

1. Do not put your life at risk. If the dog is rigid it may be fatal to touch it. Avoid touching fluids in contact with the dog.
2. Turn off electricity at source. If this is not possible, use a non-metal broom handle to move the dog well away from the exposed electric current.
3. Check whether the dog's heart is beating and it is breathing.
4. Give artificial respiration or CPR as necessary.
5. If there are only mouth burns, treat with cold compresses to reduce further damage.
6. Even if your dog recovers, get veterinary help immediately. Monitor both breathing and pulse for the next twelve hours. (Potentially fatal shock and overwhelming fluid build-up in the lungs may occur hours after an apparently uncomplicated recovery from electrocution.)

Reduce the risk of electrocution:

- Apply a bitter tasting spray to electric cords to deter puppies from chewing them
- Never leave a teething puppy in a room with live electric cords
- Examine your home environment carefully. Reposition any electric cords that may be played with by a puppy or bored dog
- Turn off electric sockets when not in use or protect them with socket covers

EYE INJURIES

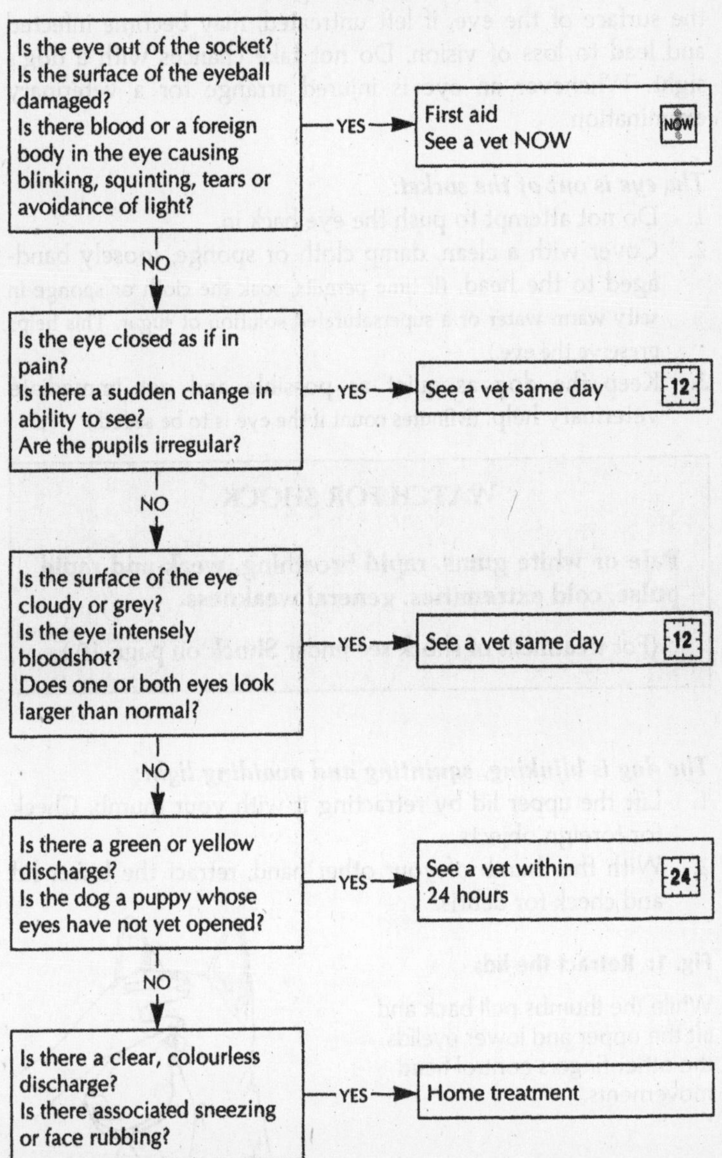
Is the eye out of the socket?
Is the surface of the eyeball damaged?
Is there blood or a foreign body in the eye causing blinking, squinting, tears or avoidance of light?
YES
First aid
See a vet NOW
NOW
NO
Is the eye closed as if in pain?
Is there a sudden change in ability to see?
Are the pupils irregular?
YES
See a vet same day
12
NO
Is the surface of the eye cloudy or grey?
Is the eye intensely bloodshot?
Does one or both eyes look larger than normal?
YES
See a vet same day
12
NO
Is there a green or yellow discharge?
Is the dog a puppy whose eyes have not yet opened?
YES
See a vet within 24 hours
24
NO
Is there a clear, colourless discharge?
Is there associated sneezing or face rubbing?
YES
Home treatment

EYE INJURIES

All eye injuries are potentially dangerous. A minor scratch to the surface of the eye, if left untreated, may become infected and lead to loss of vision. Do not take chances with a dog's sight. Whenever an eye is injured arrange for a veterinary examination.

The eye is out of the socket:

1. Do not attempt to push the eye back in.
2. Cover with a clean, damp cloth or sponge, loosely bandaged to the head. (If time permits, soak the cloth or sponge in salty warm water or a supersaturated solution of sugar. This helps preserve the eye.)
3. Keep the dog as quiet as possible and get immediate veterinary help. (Minutes count if the eye is to be saved.)

WATCH FOR SHOCK

Pale or white gums, rapid breathing, weak and rapid pulse, cold extremities, general weakness.

(For treatment of shock see under **Shock** on page 10.)

The dog is blinking, squinting and avoiding light:

1. Lift the upper lid by retracting it with your thumb. Check for foreign objects.
2. With the thumb of your other hand, retract the lower lid and check for debris.

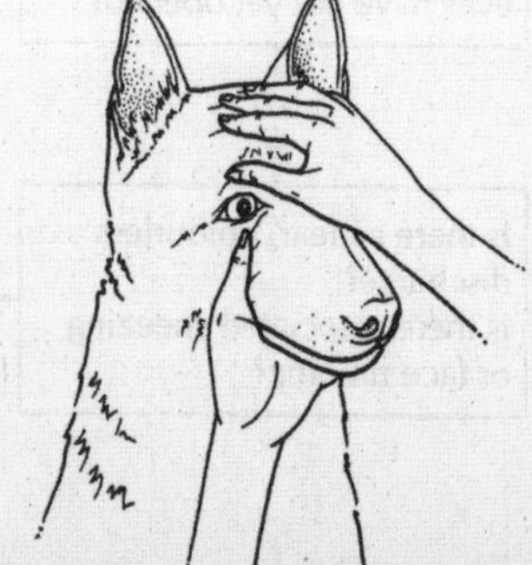

Fig. 1: Retract the lids

While the thumbs pull back and lift the upper and lower eyelids, the other fingers control head movements.

3. If there is a non-penetrating foreign object, remove it by flushing the eye with tepid water.
4. Alternatively, use a cotton swab moistened with water to ease the irritant out of the eye.

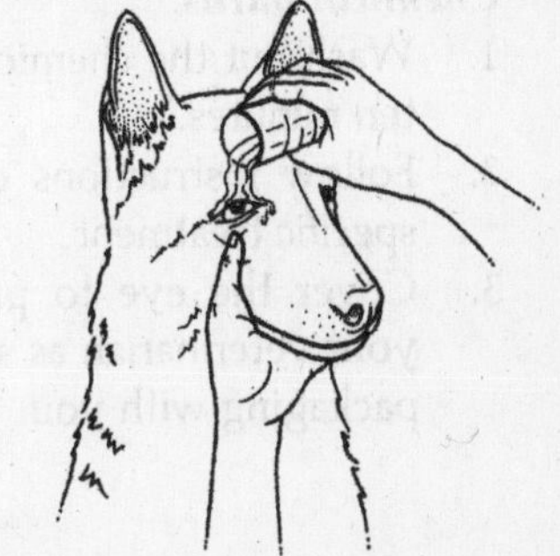

Fig. 2: Flush with water

The eye is flushed with copious fresh water to dislodge the object.

5. If you cannot remove the irritant, cover the eye with a bandage to prevent further injury and get immediate veterinary help.
6. If there is a penetrating foreign object, do not attempt to remove it. Bandage the eye or put a protective Elizabethan collar on your dog and get immediate veterinary assistance.

The eye is red, there is squinting and tear production but no foreign body:

1. If the eye has been scratched, cover it with a clean damp cloth.
2. Prevent self-inflicted damage by bandaging the eye, applying an Elizabethan collar or bandaging the dew claws.

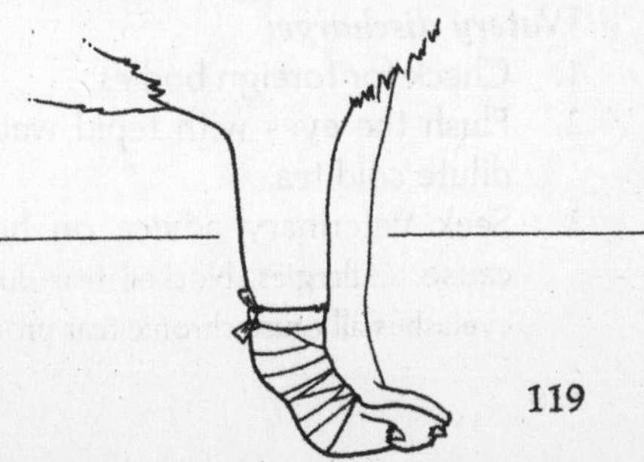

Fig. 3: Bandaged dew claws

Light bandages reduce the risk of damage from sharp dew claws if the dog paws at its eyes.

3. See your veterinarian the same day.

Chemical burns:

1. Wash out the chemical with lots of fresh water for at least ten minutes.
2. Follow instructions on the chemical packaging for more specific treatment.
3. Cover the eye to prevent self-inflicted damage and see your veterinarian as soon as possible, taking the chemical's packaging with you.

Torn, bruised or swollen eyelids from a fight or by trauma:

1. Apply a cold compress for ten minutes to reduce swelling.
2. Cover and bandage the affected lid.
3. Remove the bandage after twelve hours. See your veterinarian within twenty-four hours.
4. Use an Elizabethan collar or dew claw bandages to prevent further self-inflicted damage.

Green or yellow discharge:

1. Infection is present. Clean the eyes with tepid water, a proprietary eye wash or dilute cold tea.
2. Watch for other signs of illness and see your veterinarian within twenty-four hours.

Watery discharge:

1. Check for foreign bodies.
2. Flush the eyes with tepid water, proprietary eye wash or dilute cold tea.
3. Seek veterinary advice on how to treat the underlying cause. (Allergies, blocked tear ducts, eyelid defects or misplaced eyelashes all cause chronic tear production.)

FISH-HOOKS

Fishing lures smell delightful and often have delicacies like minnows or frogs attached to them. Unfortunately, dogs can get the hooks embedded in their lips and paws.

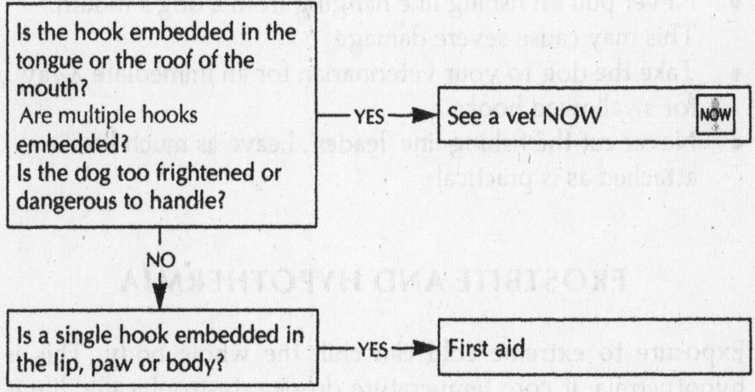
Is the hook embedded in the tongue or the roof of the mouth?
Are multiple hooks embedded?
Is the dog too frightened or dangerous to handle?
YES
See a vet NOW
NOW
NO
Is a single hook embedded in the lip, paw or body?
YES
First aid

1. Restrain and muzzle the dog, avoiding the lip area in which the hook is embedded.
2. If the barbed end of the hook is visible, cut it off with wire cutters then pull the remaining part of the hook back out in the same direction it entered.

Fig. 1: Cut the barb

If there is tension when you try to retract the hook after you have cut off the barb, stop pulling and get immediate veterinary help.

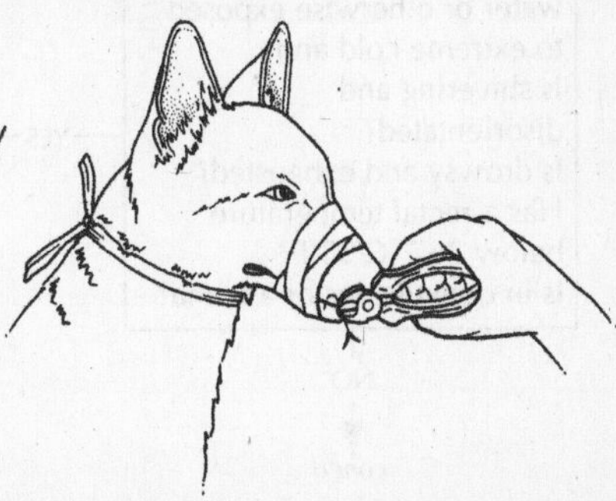

3. If the barb is not visible, use pliers to push the hook through the skin, exposing the barb.
4. Cut off the barb and retract the hook.
5. Clean the wound thoroughly with 3% hydrogen peroxide.
6. Telephone your veterinarian for further advice.

- Never pull on fishing line hanging from a dog's mouth. This may cause severe damage
- Take the dog to your veterinarian for an immediate X-ray for swallowed hooks
- Never cut the fishing line 'leader'. Leave as much line attached as is practical

FROSTBITE AND HYPOTHERMIA

Exposure to extreme cold can chill the whole body. This is hypothermia. If core temperature drops catastrophically, life is threatened. Most dogs are protected from severe cold by their dense fur. The extremities, like the tips of the ears and tail, have least protection and can suffer from local freezing or frostbite.

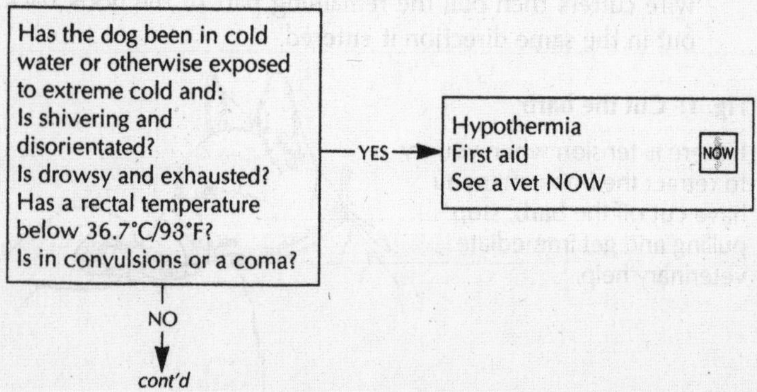
Has the dog been in cold water or otherwise exposed to extreme cold and:
Is shivering and disorientated?
Is drowsy and exhausted?
Has a rectal temperature below 36.7°C/98°F?
Is in convulsions or a coma?
YES
Hypothermia
First aid
See a vet NOW
NOW
NO
cont'd

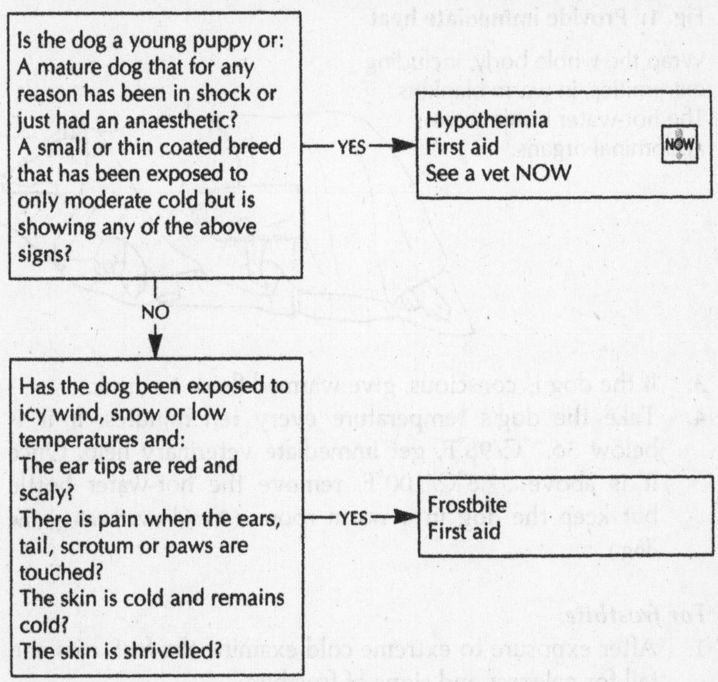
Is the dog a young puppy or:
A mature dog that for any reason has been in shock or just had an anaesthetic?
A small or thin coated breed that has been exposed to only moderate cold but is showing any of the above signs?
YES
Hypothermia
First aid
See a vet NOW
NOW
NO
Has the dog been exposed to icy wind, snow or low temperatures and:
The ear tips are red and scaly?
There is pain when the ears, tail, scrotum or paws are touched?
The skin is cold and remains cold?
The skin is shrivelled?
YES
Frostbite
First aid

WATCH FOR SHOCK

Pale or white gums, rapid breathing, weak and rapid pulse, cold extremities, general weakness.

(For treatment of shock see under **Shock** on page 10.)

For hypothermia:

1. Wrap the dog in warm blankets. (Warm the blankets quickly in your clothes drier.)
2. Place a hot-water bottle wrapped in a towel against the dog's abdomen. (Be sure to wrap the hot-water bottle. An unwrapped one will burn the skin.)

Fig. 1: Provide immediate heat

Wrap the whole body, including extremities, in warm blankets. The hot-water bottle warms abdominal organs.

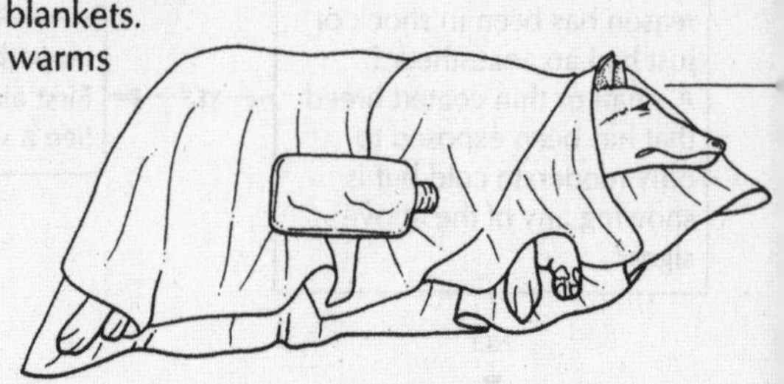

3. If the dog is conscious, give warmed fluids to drink.
4. Take the dog's temperature every ten minutes. If it is below 36.7°C/98°F, get immediate veterinary help. Once it is above 37.8°C/100°F, remove the hot-water bottle but keep the dog in a warm room. (Avoid overheating the dog.)

For frostbite:

1. After exposure to extreme cold examine the feet, ears and tail for paleness and signs of frostbite.
2. Massage the areas gently with a warm towel. (Do not rub hard or squeeze. This can further damage the affected tissue.)
3. Warm the frozen parts with tepid water heated to a maximum of 32°C/90°F. As thawing occurs, the skin becomes reddened.
4. If the skin turns dark, get immediate veterinary help.

HEART FAILURE

Sudden heart failure is uncommon in dogs, occurring most frequently in Dobermans, Great Danes and other breeds with a genetic predisposition. Progressive heart failure, also genetic, occurs in breeds such as the Cavalier King Charles spaniel and others. In most other instances, heart failure is secondary to some other major crisis. That crisis must be overcome if the dog is to survive.

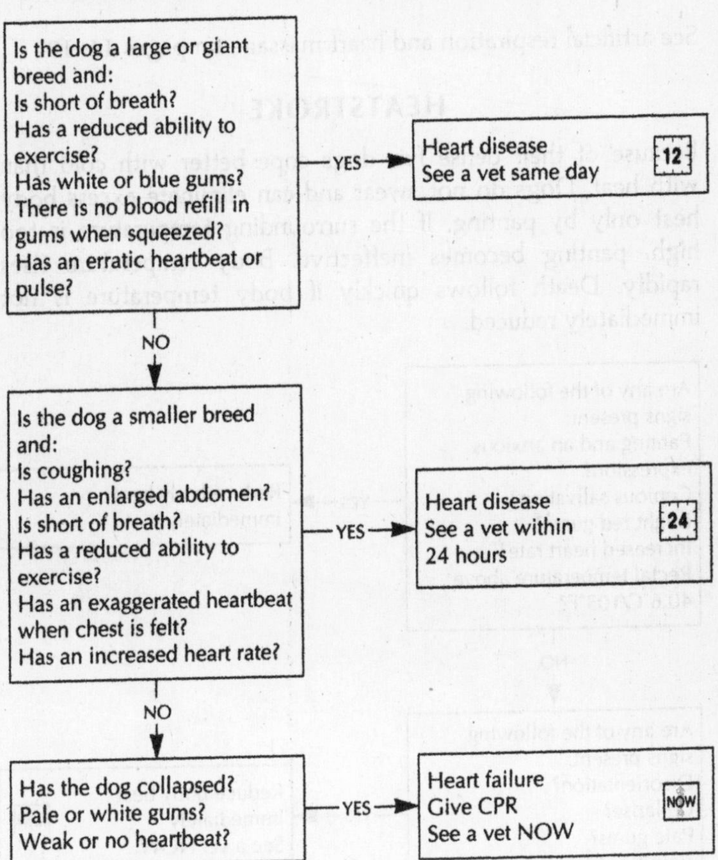
Is the dog a large or giant breed and:
Is short of breath?
Has a reduced ability to exercise?
Has white or blue gums?
There is no blood refill in gums when squeezed?
Has an erratic heartbeat or pulse?
YES
Heart disease
See a vet same day
12
NO
Is the dog a smaller breed and:
Is coughing?
Has an enlarged abdomen?
Is short of breath?
Has a reduced ability to exercise?
Has an exaggerated heartbeat when chest is felt?
Has an increased heart rate?
YES
Heart disease
See a vet within 24 hours
24
NO
Has the dog collapsed?
Pale or white gums?
Weak or no heartbeat?
YES
Heart failure
Give CPR
See a vet NOW
NOW

For heart failure:

1. Feel for a heartbeat or pulse. Squeeze the gums and see if the squeezed area refills with blood when you remove your finger.
2. If it does, the heart is still pumping. Give artificial respiration if necessary and get immediate veterinary help.

3. If the heart is not pumping, start heart massage and artificial respiration (CPR). Get immediate veterinary help.

See artificial respiration and heart massage on pages 14–18.

HEATSTROKE

Because of their dense fur, dogs cope better with cold than with heat. Dogs do not sweat and can eliminate excess body heat only by panting. If the surrounding temperature is too high, panting becomes ineffective. Body temperature rises rapidly. Death follows quickly if body temperature is not immediately reduced.

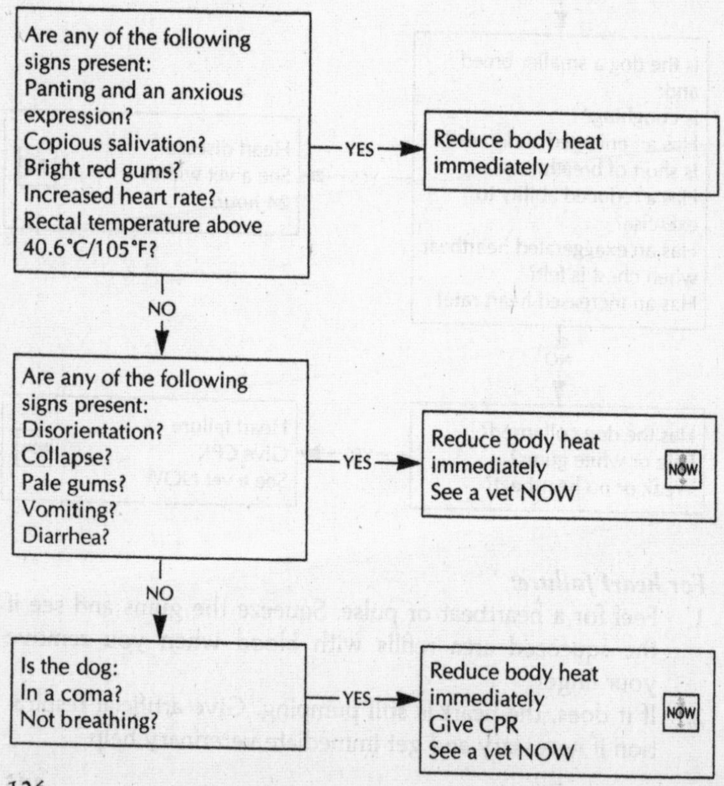
Are any of the following signs present:
Panting and an anxious expression?
Copious salivation?
Bright red gums?
Increased heart rate?
Rectal temperature above 40.6°C/105°F?
YES
Reduce body heat immediately
NO
Are any of the following signs present:
Disorientation?
Collapse?
Pale gums?
Vomiting?
Diarrhea?
YES
Reduce body heat immediately
See a vet NOW
NOW
NO
Is the dog:
In a coma?
Not breathing?
YES
Reduce body heat immediately
Give CPR
See a vet NOW
NOW

1. Remove the dog from the hot environment.
2. Put the dog in the bath. Run a cool, not ice-cold shower over the dog, directing the spray especially to the back of the neck and head, allowing water to fill the bath.

Fig. 1: Immerse in cold water

The dog's head is held above the water.

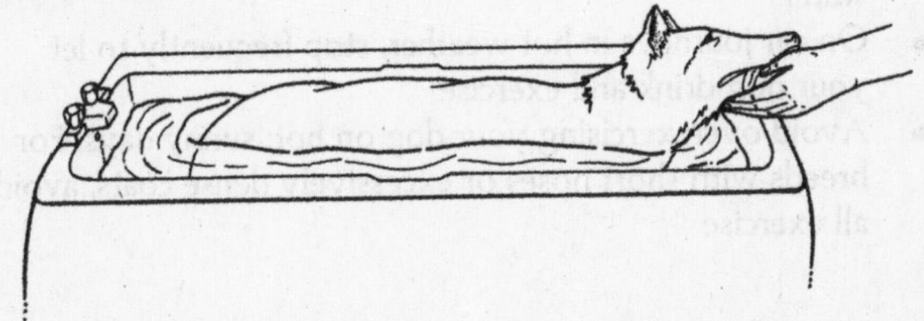

3. Alternatively, hose down the dog with a garden hose or place it in a pool of water. (Do not put the dog's head under water. If it is unconscious, make sure no water enters the nose or mouth.)
4. Apply a packet of frozen vegetables to the head to reduce heat to the brain.
5. Let the dog drink as much cold water as it wants. (A pinch of salt in the drinking water replaces salt lost through panting.)
6. Take rectal temperature every five minutes. Continue cold water immersion until the dog's temperature has fallen below 39.4°C/103°F. (Do not worry if the temperature drops down to 37.8°C/100°F or slightly less. A lower temperature is less dangerous than an extremely high one.)
7. Treat for shock if necessary and get immediate veterinary treatment. (The brain can swell causing further serious problems.)
8. Massage the legs vigorously. (This helps circulation and reduces the risk of shock.)

Do not give aspirin to reduce the dog's temperature. Aspirin can cause further problems.

Prevent heatstroke:

- Always provide your dog with good ventilation, access to shade and plenty of water to drink
- Never leave your dog in a car on a warm day
- In winter, never leave your dog in a car in direct sunlight with the heater on
- In warm weather, make sure short-nosed dogs like Pugs, old or fat dogs have access to cool rooms and plenty of water
- On car journeys in hot weather, stop frequently to let your dog drink and exercise
- Avoid overexercising your dog on hot, sunny days. For breeds with short noses or excessively dense coats, avoid all exercise

INJURIES – SURFACE

ABRASIONS – BRUISES – LACERATIONS

Injuries to the skin are common. Unpleasant abrasions occur if the skin is scraped on a hard surface. Bruises develop after more traumatic accidents when blood vessels under the skin are damaged. Skin cuts or lacerations occur most frequently to the feet, especially the pads, but can occur anywhere. If your dog shows signs of these superficial injuries, carry out a complete examination for potentially more serious, deeper damage.

WATCH FOR SHOCK

Pale or white gums, rapid breathing, weak and rapid pulse, cold extremities, general weakness.

(For treatment of shock see under **Shock** on page 10.)

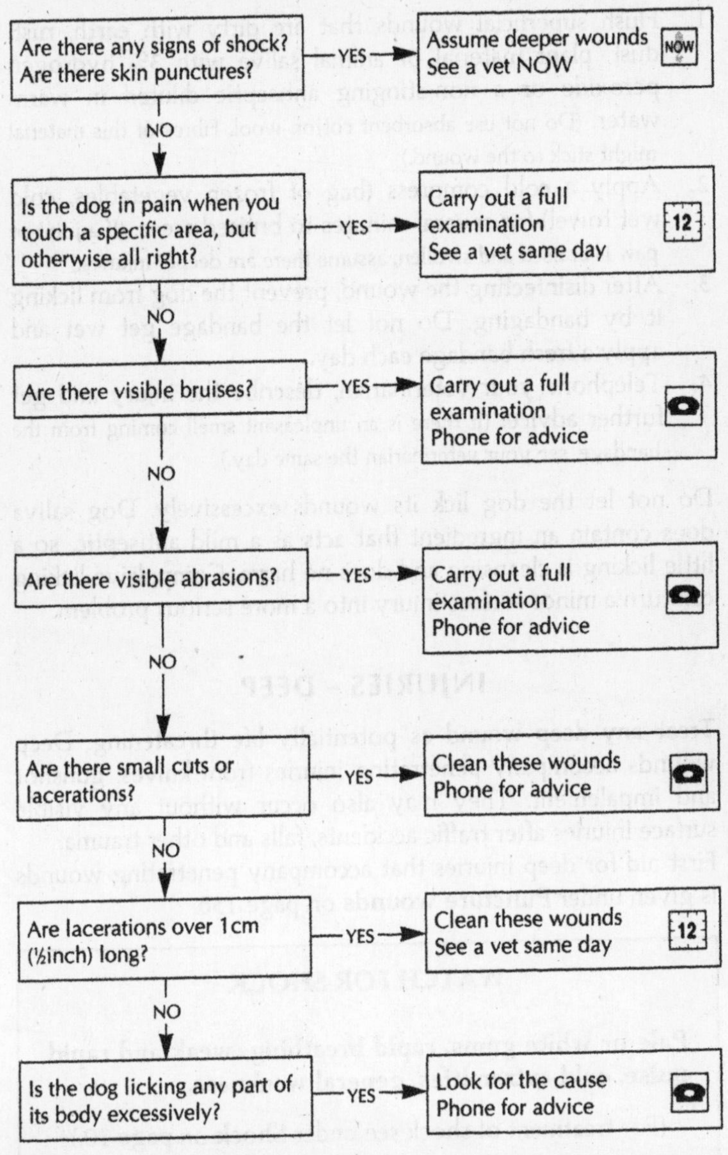
Are there any signs of shock?
Are there skin punctures?
YES
Assume deeper wounds
See a vet NOW
NOW
NO
Is the dog in pain when you touch a specific area, but otherwise all right?
YES
Carry out a full examination
See a vet same day
12
NO
Are there visible bruises?
YES
Carry out a full examination
Phone for advice
NO
Are there visible abrasions?
YES
Carry out a full examination
Phone for advice
NO
Are there small cuts or lacerations?
YES
Clean these wounds
Phone for advice
NO
Are lacerations over 1cm (½inch) long?
YES
Clean these wounds
See a vet same day
12
NO
Is the dog licking any part of its body excessively?
YES
Look for the cause
Phone for advice

1. Flush superficial wounds that are dirty with earth, rust, dust, plant material or animal saliva with 3% hydrogen peroxide or a non-stinging antiseptic diluted in warm water. (Do not use absorbent cotton wool. Fibres of this material might stick to the wound.)
2. Apply a cold compress (bag of frozen vegetables, cold wet towel) for several minutes to bruised areas. (If a joint or paw is bruised and swollen, assume there are deeper injuries.)
3. After disinfecting the wound, prevent the dog from licking it by bandaging. Do not let the bandage get wet and apply a fresh bandage each day.
4. Telephone your veterinarian, describe the injury and get further advice. (If there is an unpleasant smell coming from the bandage, see your veterinarian the same day.)

Do not let the dog lick its wounds excessively. Dog saliva does contain an ingredient that acts as a mild antiseptic, so a little licking is cleansing and does no harm. Compulsive licking can turn a minor surface injury into a more serious problem.

INJURIES – DEEP

Treat any deep wound as potentially life threatening. Deep wounds accompany penetrating injuries from knives, gunshot and impalement. They may also occur without any visible surface injuries after traffic accidents, falls and other trauma.
First aid for deep injuries that accompany penetrating wounds is given under **Puncture wounds** on page 156.

WATCH FOR SHOCK

Pale or white gums, rapid breathing, weak and rapid pulse, cold extremities, general weakness.

(For treatment of shock see under **Shock** on page 10.)

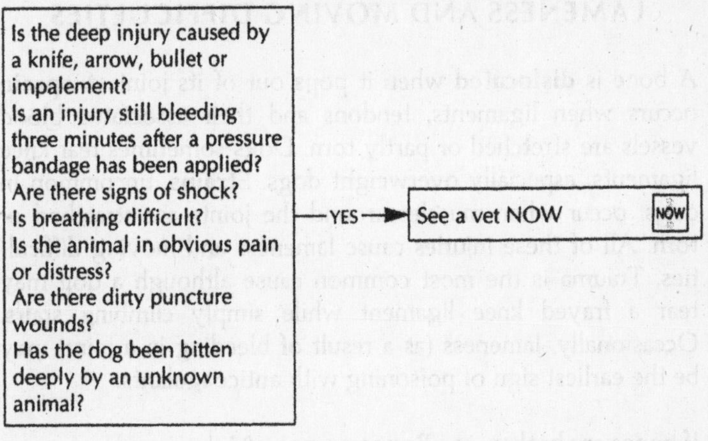
Is the deep injury caused by a knife, arrow, bullet or impalement?
Is an injury still bleeding three minutes after a pressure bandage has been applied?
Are there signs of shock?
Is breathing difficult?
Is the animal in obvious pain or distress?
Are there dirty puncture wounds?
Has the dog been bitten deeply by an unknown animal?
YES
See a vet NOW
NOW

1. Do not remove any penetrating objects such as arrows. (Removal may cause fatal internal bleeding. Always try to move the dog **with** the article it has impaled itself on. If this is not possible, try to get on-site immediate veterinary help. If this cannot be done, be prepared for possible fatal consequences when the dog is removed from the impaling object.
2. Calm the dog, apply pressure to control bleeding. Keep the airway open.
3. Give CPR if necessary.
4. Assume that shock will occur. Wrap the dog in a blanket to keep it warm and get immediate veterinary help.

Remember, deep injuries such as concussion, torn diaphragms, ruptured bladders and hemorrhages from torn organs or blood vessels can occur without any visible superficial damage. If you know your dog has had a traumatic accident or if you see signs of shock while giving a head-to-tail examination after you have found signs of superficial injuries, get immediate veterinary help.

See under **Puncture wounds** on page 156 for further information.

LAMENESS AND MOVING DIFFICULTIES

A bone is **dislocated** when it pops out of its joint. A **sprain** occurs when ligaments, tendons and their associated blood vessels are stretched or partly torn. Dogs sometimes tear knee ligaments, especially overweight dogs. **Strains**, uncommon in dogs, occur when muscles around the joints are stretched or torn. All of these injuries cause lameness and moving difficulties. Trauma is the most common cause although a dog may tear a frayed knee ligament while simply climbing stairs. Occasionally, lameness (as a result of bleeding in a joint) may be the earliest sign of poisoning with anticoagulants.

If bones are broken, see **Bones** on page 83.

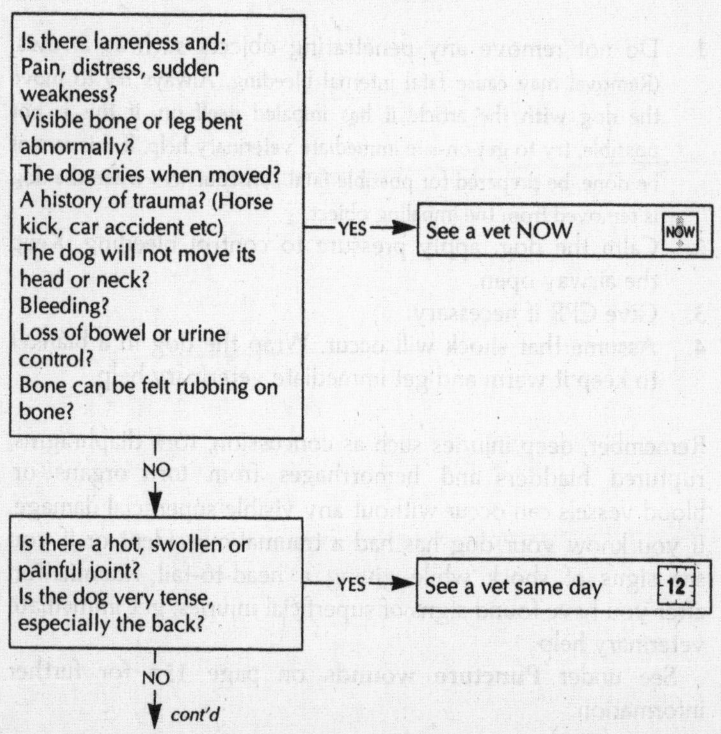
Is there lameness and:
Pain, distress, sudden weakness?
Visible bone or leg bent abnormally?
The dog cries when moved?
A history of trauma? (Horse kick, car accident etc)
The dog will not move its head or neck?
Bleeding?
Loss of bowel or urine control?
Bone can be felt rubbing on bone?
YES
See a vet NOW
NOW
NO
Is there a hot, swollen or painful joint?
Is the dog very tense, especially the back?
YES
See a vet same day
12
NO
cont'd

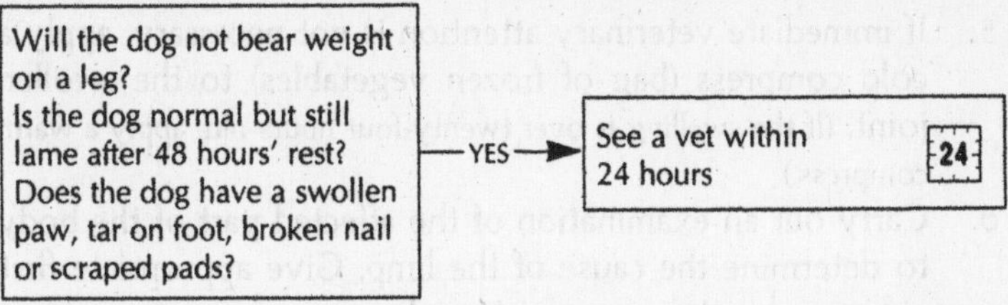
Will the dog not bear weight on a leg?
Is the dog normal but still lame after 48 hours' rest?
Does the dog have a swollen paw, tar on foot, broken nail or scraped pads?
YES
See a vet within 24 hours
24

WATCH FOR SHOCK

Pale or white gums, rapid breathing, weak and rapid pulse, cold extremities, general weakness.

(For treatment of shock see under Shock on page 10.)

1. Restrain the dog if necessary and move it as little as possible.
2. If there are no obvious fractures and the dog can walk, do not attempt to splint the leg.
3. If there is severe pain or swelling, allow a large dog to walk on three legs to the car and get immediate veterinary help. Gently carry small dogs.
4. Cradle the back of dogs with back pain.

Fig. 1: Support the back

Keep the dog's back straight by supporting its weight in front of the shoulders and behind the hips.

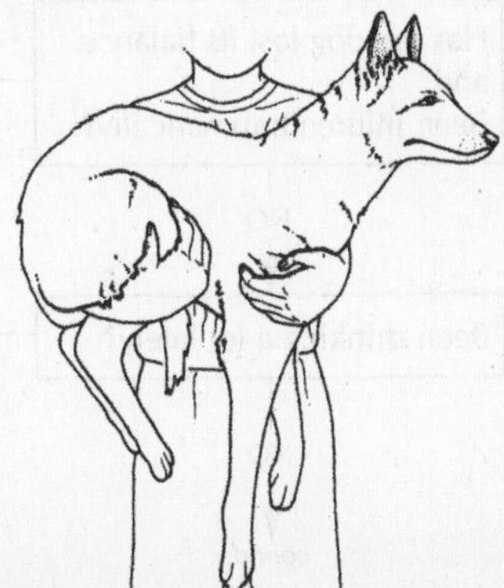

5. If immediate veterinary attention is not necessary, apply a cold compress (bag of frozen vegetables) to the swollen joint. (If the swelling is over twenty-four hours old, apply a warm compress.)
6. Carry out an examination of the affected part of the body to determine the cause of the limp. Give appropriate first aid or seek veterinary assistance.
7. Always provide absolute rest – no exercise – for lame dogs.

Lameness does not tell us what is wrong, it only reveals the presence of damage that is causing pain. Always continue resting lame dogs for at least twenty-four hours **after** lameness has disappeared. Reintroduce exercise gradually.

LOSS OF BALANCE

Sudden loss of balance may be caused by the early stages of brain concussion, by diabetic crisis, by shock or by spreading ear or throat infection. In older dogs it may be due to a brain disorder affecting the balance (vestibular) center. Poisoning by swallowing human medications, illicit mind-altering drugs or alcohol can also cause loss of balance.

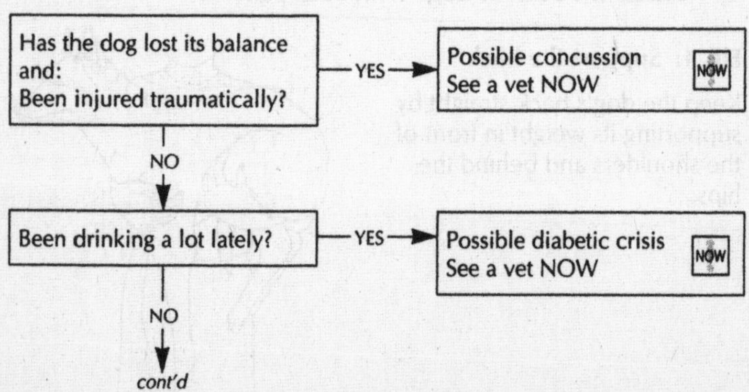
Has the dog lost its balance and:
Been injured traumatically?
YES
Possible concussion
See a vet NOW
NOW
NO
Been drinking a lot lately?
YES
Possible diabetic crisis
See a vet NOW
NOW
NO
cont'd

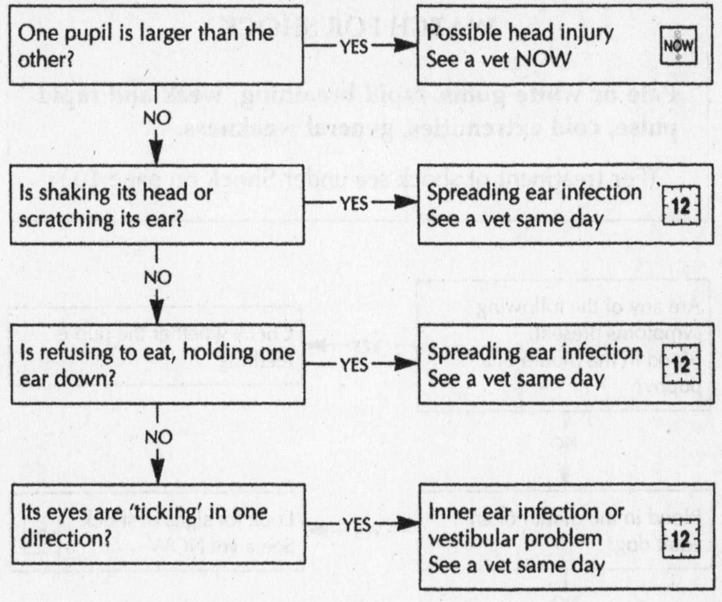
One pupil is larger than the other?
YES
Possible head injury
See a vet NOW
NOW
NO
Is shaking its head or scratching its ear?
YES
Spreading ear infection
See a vet same day
12
NO
Is refusing to eat, holding one ear down?
YES
Spreading ear infection
See a vet same day
12
NO
Its eyes are 'ticking' in one direction?
YES
Inner ear infection or vestibular problem
See a vet same day
12

1. Prevent the dog from falling and injuring itself.
2. Look for signs of head injuries that indicate trauma. Get immediate veterinary attention if there are signs of injury or shock.
3. Examine the ears for wax, inflammation or discharge – all signs of external ear infection that can move to the inner ear and cause loss of balance. Get veterinary help the same day.

MOUTH INJURIES

A dog should not drool, should not avoid food when it is hungry, should chew, lap water and swallow normally, and show no signs of pain when its jaws are opened or its mouth touched. Mouth odor should not be repellent.

WATCH FOR SHOCK

Pale or white gums, rapid breathing, weak and rapid pulse, cold extremities, general weakness.

(For treatment of shock see under **Shock** on page 10.)

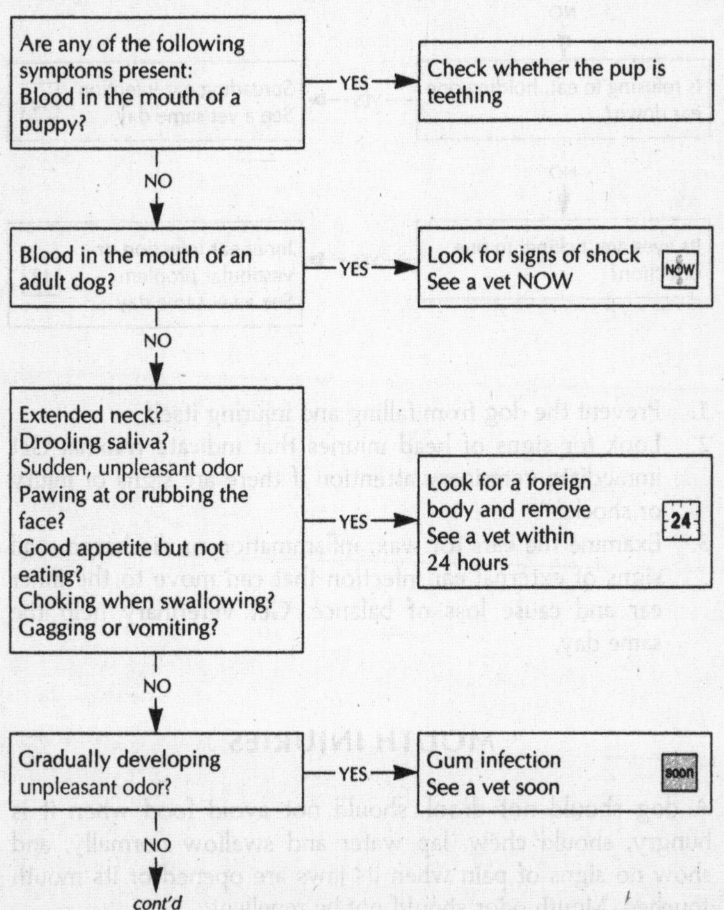

Are any of the following symptoms present: Blood in the mouth of a puppy?
YES
Check whether the pup is teething
NO
Blood in the mouth of an adult dog?
YES
Look for signs of shock See a vet NOW
NOW
NO
Extended neck? Drooling saliva? Sudden, unpleasant odor Pawing at or rubbing the face? Good appetite but not eating? Choking when swallowing? Gagging or vomiting?
YES
Look for a foreign body and remove See a vet within 24 hours
24
NO
Gradually developing unpleasant odor?
YES
Gum infection See a vet soon
soon
NO
cont'd

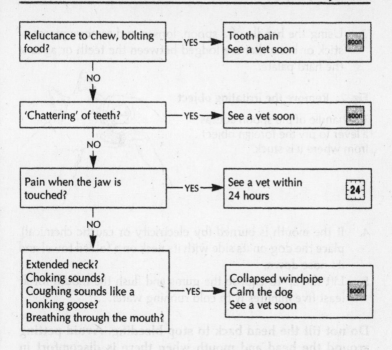

Reluctance to chew, bolting food?	YES →	Tooth pain See a vet soon (soon)
NO ↓		
'Chattering' of teeth?	YES →	See a vet soon (soon)
NO ↓		
Pain when the jaw is touched?	YES →	See a vet within 24 hours (24)
NO ↓		
Extended neck? Choking sounds? Coughing sounds like a honking goose? Breathing through the mouth?	YES →	Collapsed windpipe Calm the dog See a vet soon (soon)

1. In good light, open the mouth and examine the teeth and hard palate.

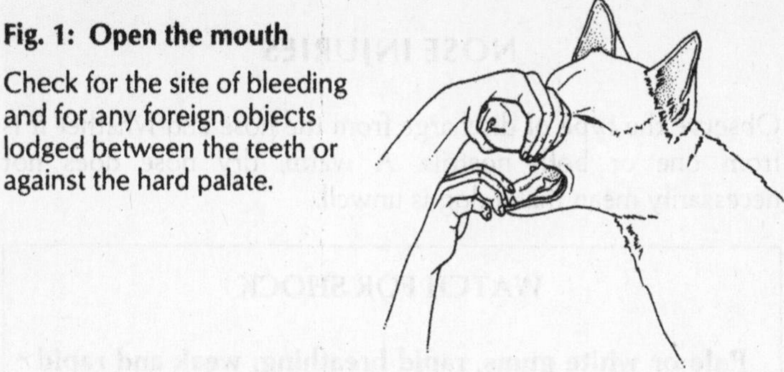

Fig. 1: Open the mouth

Check for the site of bleeding and for any foreign objects lodged between the teeth or against the hard palate.

2. Apply a cold compress to any accessible bleeding site. Look for signs of shock.

3. Using the handle of a spoon, loosen and remove pieces of stick or bone that are lodged between the teeth or against the hard palate.

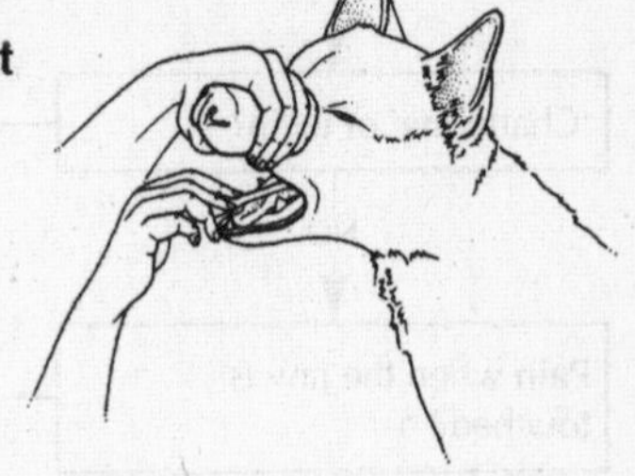

Fig. 2: Remove the irritating object

The handle of the spoon acts as a lever to pry the foreign object from where it is stuck.

4. If the mouth is burned (by electricity or caustic chemical), place the dog on its side with its neck on a folded towel and its nose down.
5. Lift the lip to expose the gums and flush the mouth for at least five minutes with cold running water.

Do not tilt the head back to stop bleeding. Avoid petting around the head and mouth when there is discomfort in the mouth.

NOSE INJURIES

Observe the type of discharge from the nose and whether it is from one or both nostrils. A warm, dry nose does not necessarily mean that a dog is unwell.

WATCH FOR SHOCK

Pale or white gums, rapid breathing, weak and rapid pulse, cold extremities, general weakness.

(For treatment of shock see under **Shock** on page 10.)

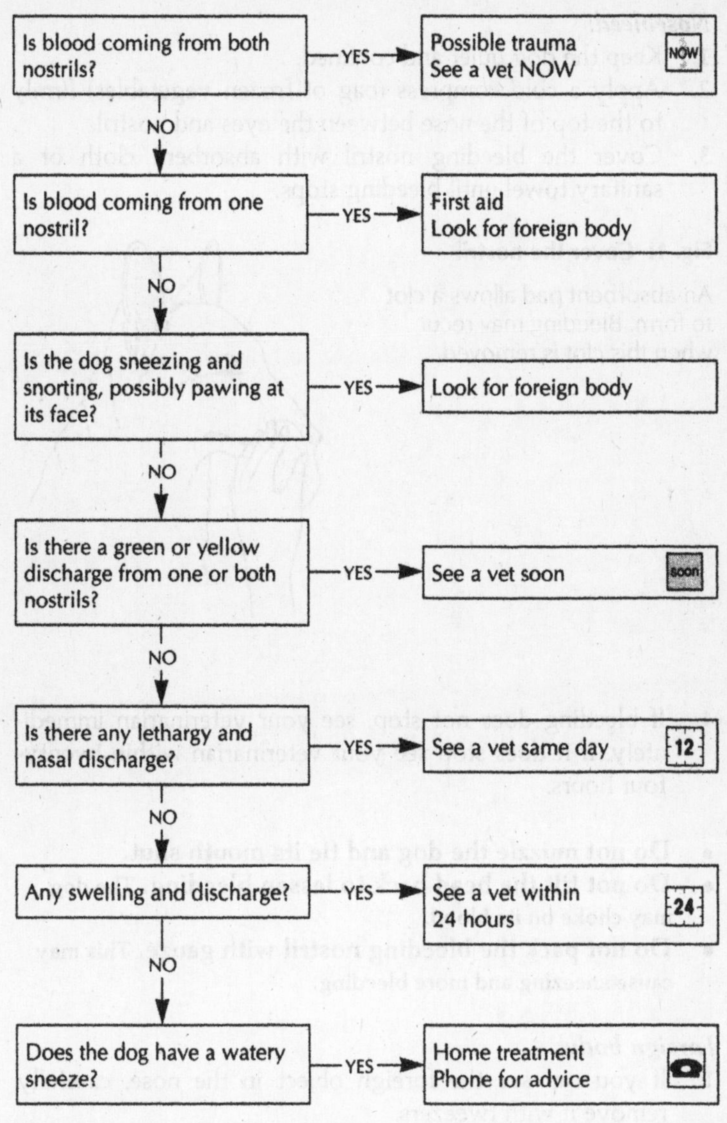
Is blood coming from both nostrils?
YES
Possible trauma
See a vet NOW
NOW
NO
Is blood coming from one nostril?
YES
First aid
Look for foreign body
NO
Is the dog sneezing and snorting, possibly pawing at its face?
YES
Look for foreign body
NO
Is there a green or yellow discharge from one or both nostrils?
YES
See a vet soon
soon
NO
Is there any lethargy and nasal discharge?
YES
See a vet same day
12
NO
Any swelling and discharge?
YES
See a vet within 24 hours
24
NO
Does the dog have a watery sneeze?
YES
Home treatment
Phone for advice

Nosebleed:

1. Keep the dog quiet and confined.
2. Apply a cold compress (bag of frozen vegetables) firmly to the top of the nose between the eyes and nostrils.
3. Cover the bleeding nostril with absorbent cloth or a sanitary towel until bleeding stops.

Fig. 1: Cover the nostril

An absorbent pad allows a clot to form. Bleeding may recur when this clot is removed.

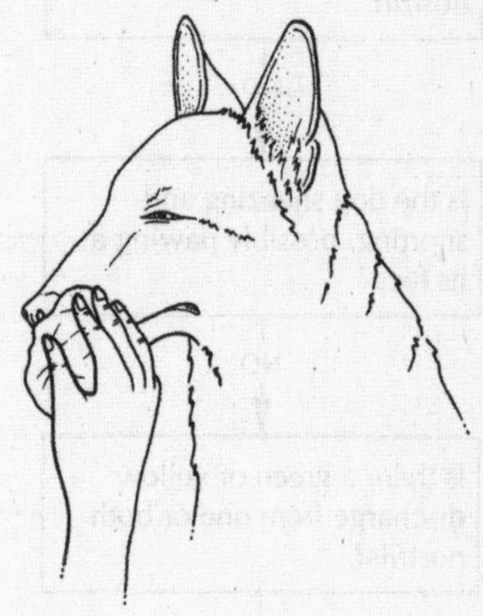

4. If bleeding does not stop, see your veterinarian immediately. If it does stop see your veterinarian within twenty-four hours.

- **Do not muzzle the dog and tie its mouth shut.**
- **Do not tilt the head back to lessen bleeding. The dog may choke on its blood.**
- **Do not pack the bleeding nostril with gauze. This may cause sneezing and more bleeding.**

Foreign body:

1. If you can see the foreign object in the nose, carefully remove it with tweezers.
2. If you cannot see the foreign object or cannot remove it, take your dog to your veterinarian the same day.

POISON – SKIN CONTACT

Paint, paint remover, tar, petroleum products, motor oil and many other chemicals can all cause irritating skin damage and burns. If the dog licks these substances, the inside of the mouth may be burned. If they are swallowed, general poisoning may result. Do not assume that dogs are resistant to the irritation of stinging nettles. Short-haired dogs in particular are susceptible to intense discomfort. Some hunting dogs have died of shock after exposure to nettles.

WATCH FOR SHOCK

Pale or white gums, rapid breathing, weak and rapid pulse, cold extremities, general weakness.

(For treatment of shock see under Shock on page 10.)

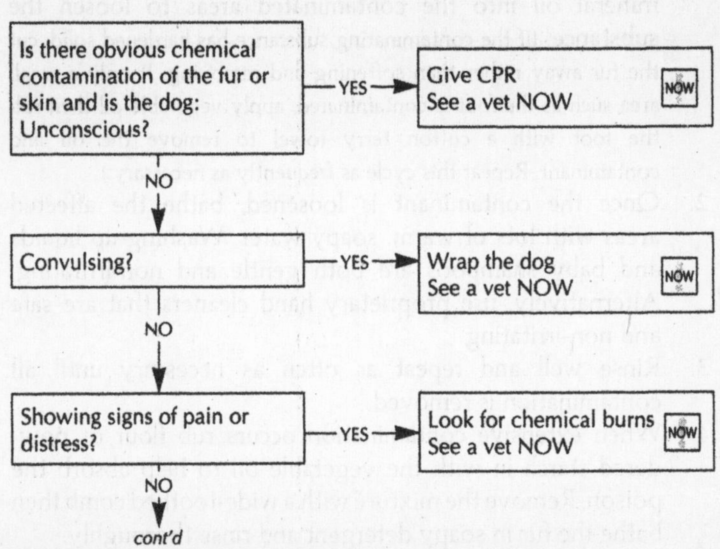
Is there obvious chemical contamination of the fur or skin and is the dog: Unconscious?
YES
Give CPR
See a vet NOW
NOW
NO
Convulsing?
YES
Wrap the dog
See a vet NOW
NOW
NO
Showing signs of pain or distress?
YES
Look for chemical burns
See a vet NOW
NOW
NO
cont'd

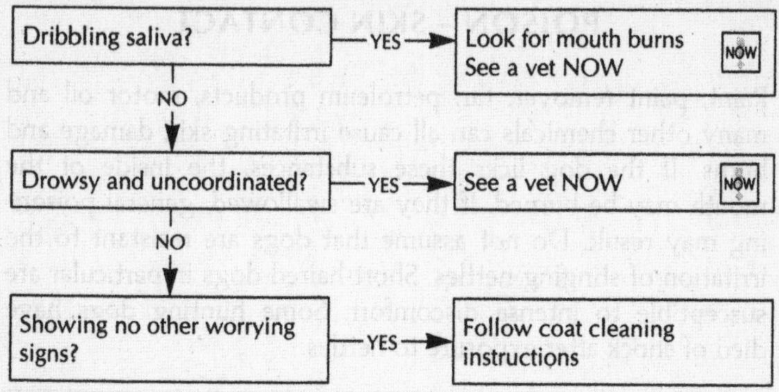
Dribbling saliva?
YES
Look for mouth burns
See a vet NOW
NOW
NO
Drowsy and uncoordinated?
YES
See a vet NOW
NOW
NO
Showing no other worrying signs?
YES
Follow coat cleaning instructions

If the dog's coat is contaminated with paint, tar or motor oil:

Do not use paint stripper, paint brush cleaner, paint thinner, turpentine, turpentine substitute or mineral spirits. Do not use concentrated biological detergents.

1. Wearing rubber gloves, rub large amounts of vegetable or mineral oil into the contaminated areas to loosen the substance. (If the contaminating substance has hardened solid, cut the fur away rather than softening and removing. If only a small area such as the foot is contaminated, apply vegetable oil then rub the foot with a cotton terry towel to remove the oil and contaminant. Repeat this cycle as frequently as necessary.)
2. Once the contaminant is loosened, bathe the affected areas with lots of warm, soapy water. Washing-up liquids and baby shampoos are both gentle and non-irritating. Alternatively, use proprietary hand cleaners that are safe and non-irritating.
3. Rinse well and repeat as often as necessary until all contamination is removed.
4. When extensive contamination occurs rub flour or powdered starch in with the vegetable oil to help absorb the poison. Remove the mixture with a wide-toothed comb then bathe the fur in soapy detergent and rinse thoroughly.

If the dog's coat is contaminated by anything other than paint, tar, petroleum products and motor oil:

1. Flush the contaminated area for at least five minutes with large quantities of clean water.
2. Wearing gloves, wash the affected areas with warm, soapy water, mild detergent such as baby shampoo or washing-up liquid.

If your dog has been exposed to stinging nettles:

1. Watch for signs of shock.
2. Give an antihistamine by mouth.
3. Wash the affected areas such as the groin with soapy water or mild detergent.
4. Offer lots of food and water.
5. Keep your dog active and alert.
6. If pain is intense or there are signs of shock, see your veterinarian immediately.

POISON – INHALED

Inhaled poisons most often interfere with breathing. Others, concentrated insecticide fumes for example, may cause neurological signs like twitching and salivating. If smoke or irritants such as tear gas have been inhaled, assume that the air passages will be inflamed.

Do not put yourself at risk by entering an environment containing dangerous toxic fumes.

WATCH FOR SHOCK

Pale or white gums, rapid breathing, weak and rapid pulse, cold extremities, general weakness.

(For treatment of shock see under **Shock** on page 10.)

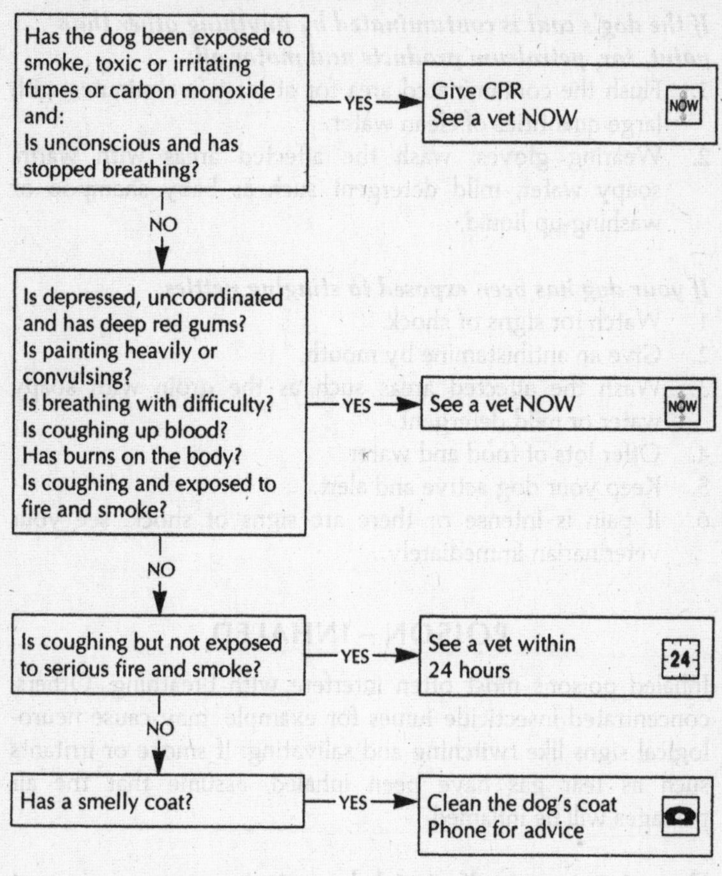
Has the dog been exposed to smoke, toxic or irritating fumes or carbon monoxide and:
Is unconscious and has stopped breathing?
YES
Give CPR
See a vet NOW
NOW
NO
Is depressed, uncoordinated and has deep red gums?
Is painting heavily or convulsing?
Is breathing with difficulty?
Is coughing up blood?
Has burns on the body?
Is coughing and exposed to fire and smoke?
YES
See a vet NOW
NOW
NO
Is coughing but not exposed to serious fire and smoke?
YES
See a vet within 24 hours
24
NO
Has a smelly coat?
YES
Clean the dog's coat
Phone for advice

1. For all inhalation poisonings, keep the dog's airway open, maintain breathing and assist circulation by giving CPR when necessary.
2. If the dog is convulsing, wrap it in a blanket.
3. Get immediate veterinary help.
4. If there is time to do so, flush the dog's eyes with lots of fresh water or proprietary eyewash.

Do not underestimate the damage caused by inhaling

smoke or other irritant fumes. Serious and potentially fatal swelling may affect the air passages hours later. After any serious inhalation accident always get veterinary advice and assistance.

POISON – SWALLOWED

Dogs have fairly non-discriminatory taste buds. An unfortunate consequence is that they are prone to poisoning themselves by eating harmful substances. Some poisons cause unpleasant but temporary side effects. Others may be fatal within an hour unless antidotes and veterinary attention is given.

WATCH FOR SHOCK

Pale or white gums, rapid breathing, weak and rapid pulse, cold extremities, general weakness.

(For treatment of shock see under **Shock** on page 10.)

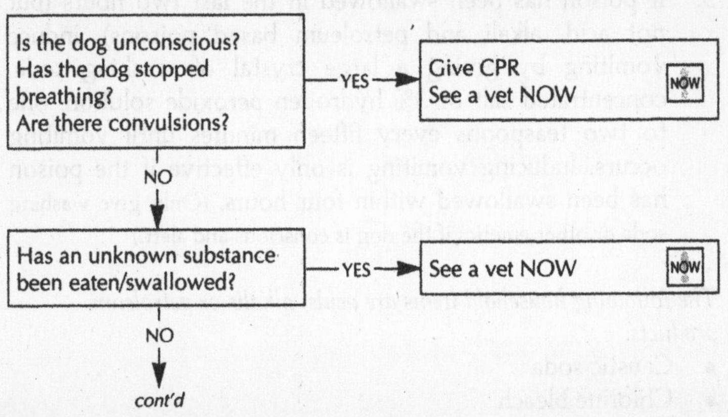
Is the dog unconscious?
Has the dog stopped breathing?
Are there convulsions?
YES
Give CPR
See a vet NOW
NOW
NO
Has an unknown substance been eaten/swallowed?
YES
See a vet NOW
NOW
NO
cont'd

POISON – SWALLOWED

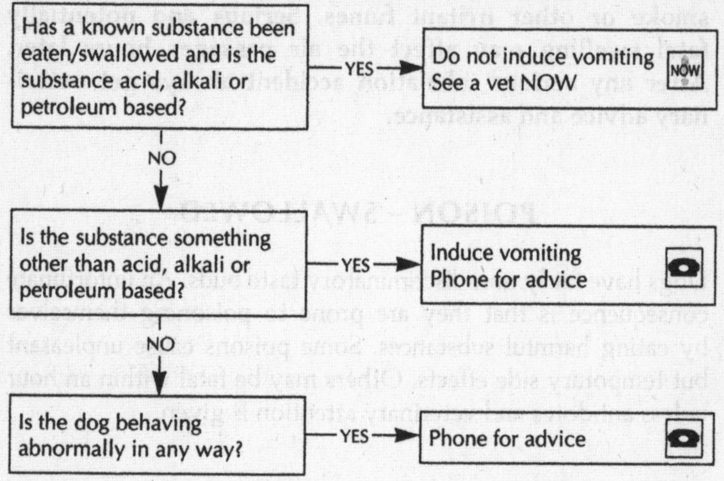

Has a known substance been eaten/swallowed and is the substance acid, alkali or petroleum based?
YES
Do not induce vomiting
See a vet NOW
NOW
NO
Is the substance something other than acid, alkali or petroleum based?
YES
Induce vomiting
Phone for advice
NO
Is the dog behaving abnormally in any way?
YES
Phone for advice

1. Do not panic. If shock has developed or the dog is unconscious, keep the airway open, maintain breathing and circulation and see your veterinarian immediately.
2. If convulsions have developed, prevent the dog from damaging itself or from biting you and others and get immediate veterinary help. Prevent overheating by not covering the dog during transport.
3. If poison has been swallowed in the last two hours (but not acid, alkali and petroleum based poisons), induce vomiting by giving a large crystal of washing soda, concentrated salt or 3% hydrogen peroxide solution, one to two teaspoons every fifteen minutes until vomiting occurs. Inducing vomiting is only effective if the poison has been swallowed within four hours. (Only give washing soda or other emetics if the dog is conscious and alert.)

The following household items are acids, alkalis or petroleum products:

- Caustic soda
- Chlorine bleach

- Dishwasher granules
- Drain cleaner
- Kerosene
- Laundry detergents
- Lye
- Oven cleaner
- Paint stripper and remover
- Paint thinner
- Gasoline
- Polishes – furniture, floor and shoe
- Toilet cleaner
- Wood preservatives

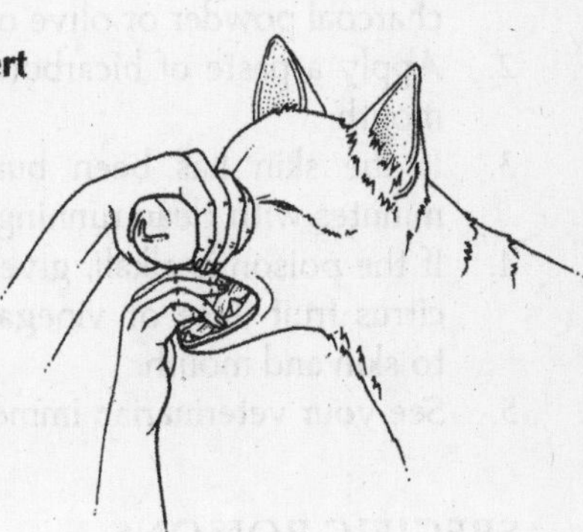

Fig. 1: Open the mouth and insert washing soda

One hand lifts the upper jaw, squeezing the upper lips over the teeth. The other hand puts the washing soda crystal or ball of salt over the hump of the tongue.

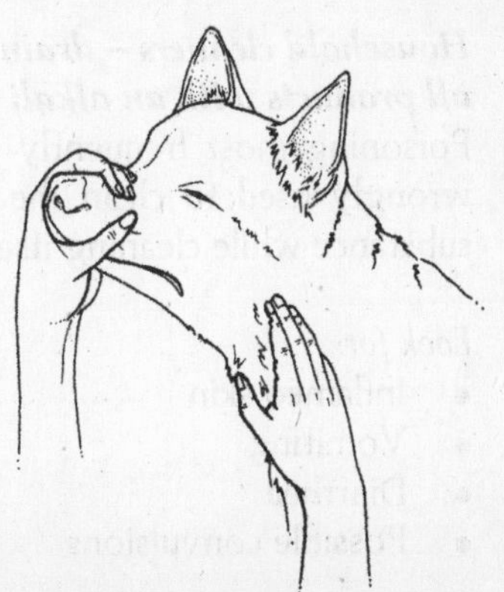

Fig. 2: Hold the mouth shut

One hand keeps the dog's mouth shut. The other strokes the neck. When the dog licks its lips it has swallowed the emetic. Vomiting occurs within several minutes.

4. Give one to two teaspoons of a suspension of activated charcoal in water. (This helps absorb any remaining poison.)
5. If the poison is unknown, do not throw out the vomit. Keep a sample to take to your veterinarian. See your veterinarian as soon as possible.
6. If the poison is known, telephone your veterinarian or poison control center for advice.
7. If any signs of poisoning develop, give first aid and transport the dog to the veterinarian as soon as possible.

If an alkali, acid or petroleum based poison is swallowed, do not induce vomiting:

1. If the poison is acid, give egg white, bicarbonate of soda, charcoal powder or olive oil by mouth.
2. Apply a paste of bicarbonate of soda to any burns in the mouth.
3. If the skin has been burned, flush for at least fifteen minutes with clean running water.
4. If the poison is alkali, give egg white or small amounts of citrus fruit juice or vinegar. Pour vinegar on alkali burns to skin and mouth.
5. See your veterinarian immediately.

SPECIFIC POISONS

Household cleaners – drain cleaner, solvents, paint stripper, all products with an alkali or acid symbol on labels

Poisoning most frequently occurs when these substances are wrongly used to clean the dog's fur. The dog swallows the substance while cleaning itself.

Look for:

- Inflamed skin
- Vomiting
- Diarrhea
- Possible convulsions

- Depression
- Coughing
- Abdominal pain
- Redness in the mouth and on the tongue

1. Do not induce vomiting.
2. Give between one and three tablespoons of olive oil or similar vegetable oil orally, according to the dog's size.
3. Wash the skin and coat thoroughly with soapy water. (Wear rubber gloves to avoid burning your own skin. See **Poison – skin contact** on page 141).
4. Get immediate veterinary help.

Insecticides – flea collars, concentrated washes, shampoos, sprays containing organophosphates and carbamates

Poisoning occurs most commonly when a dog eats a flea collar or licks insecticide off its coat.

Look for:

CARBAMATES:

- Agitation
- Restlessness
- Twitching
- Salivation
- Convulsions
- Coma

ORGANOPHOSPHATES:

- Hind leg weakness
- Breathing difficulties
- Muscle tremors
- Salivation
- Increased urinating / defecating

1. Provide first aid according to the needs of the dog.
2. If consumed, induce vomiting and give activated charcoal.
3. If there is skin contact, wash off remaining insecticide with soapy water. (Wear rubber gloves to protect yourself from exposure.)
4. Get immediate veterinary help.

Rodent poison

Many different types of rodenticide are available. Check the packaging to find out the chemical name of the poison. The dog may be poisoned by the bait itself or by eating the poisoned rodent.

Warfarin
Look for:

- Vomiting
- Lethargy
- Signs of internal bleeding
- Pale gums and signs of shock
- Bruising to the skin

1. If the dog has just eaten warfarin, induce vomiting then give activated charcoal by mouth.
2. If the dog shows signs of poisoning, keep the dog warm, treat for shock and take the dog and a sample of the rodenticide or the packaging to the veterinarian as soon as possible. (Vitamin K, given by injection, is a specific antidote for warfarin poisoning.)
3. Warfarin is especially dangerous to small dogs. It may be fatal.

Strychnine
Look for:

- A worried look
- Tenseness and stiffness leading to convulsions

Can be fatal within an hour.

1. Induce vomiting only if breathing is regular and give activated charcoal.
2. Get immediate veterinary help.

Sodium fluoroacetate
Look for:

- Initial excitement followed by depression
- Convulsions

- Vomiting
- Urinating and repeated bowel motions

1. Induce vomiting and give activated charcoal by mouth.
2. Keep the dog warm.
3. Get immediate veterinary help.

Slug and snail bait – metaldehyde

Dogs enjoy the taste of metaldehyde and willingly eat it. This may be fatal.

Look for:

- Tremors
- Salivation
- Convulsions
- Coma

1. If recently swallowed, induce vomiting with soda crystals, 3% hydrogen peroxide or a ball of salt.
2. Do not let the dog get overheated. See your veterinarian as soon as possible. (Treatment may involve prolonged anaesthesia.)

Antifreeze – ethylene glycol

Dogs enjoy the taste of antifreeze that has leaked from car radiators. Newer types of antifreeze are not toxic. Ethylene glycol poisoning can be fatal.

Look for:

- Wobbling
- Convulsions
- Vomiting
- Collapse
- Coma

1. If recently swallowed, induce vomiting and give activated charcoal by mouth.

2. Get veterinary attention urgently.
3. If veterinary treatment is a great distance away, give small amounts of alcohol by mouth. (This reduces ethylene glycol damage to the kidneys.)

Aspirin

Poisoning occurs most commonly as a result of the dog being given aspirin to relieve pain.

Look for:

- Poor appetite
- Depression
- Abdominal cramp
- Vomiting with or without blood
- Uncoordination

1. Induce vomiting with baking soda crystals. (This also counteracts the poisoning effect of aspirin.)
2. Give no other medicines.
3. Telephone your veterinarian for further advice.

Illicit drugs

Dogs either find illicit drugs such as cannabis or ecstasy accidentally or are sometimes given them.

Look for:

- Uncoordination
- Agitation
- Fear biting
- Dilated pupils

1. Avoid any unnecessary sensory stimulation such as light and sound.
2. Get immediate veterinary attention.

Sedatives, antidepressants and antianxiety drugs

These prescription medicines are either discovered by or intentionally given to the dog.

Look for:

- Depression
- Staggering
- Restlessness or agitation
- Rapid heartbeat or heart palpitations
- Deep sleep or coma

1. If the dog has just swallowed the pills, induce vomiting with a washing soda crystal, 3% hydrogen peroxide or a ball of salt. Feed activated charcoal.
2. Keep the dog warm. Talk to it constantly.
3. Give first aid if the dog is slipping into a coma.
4. Telephone your veterinarian for advice.

Battery acid

Dogs sometimes chew on old car batteries or lap up car battery acid, burning their mouths and causing internal poisoning.

Look for:

- Burns to the mouth and skin
- Vomiting, sometimes with blood
- Shock

1. Do not induce vomiting.
2. Treat for shock if it has developed.
3. Give bicarbonate of soda in water orally.
4. Get immediate veterinary attention.

Chlorine

Occasionally dogs poison themselves by chewing on chlorine tablets used to purify swimming pools. Chlorine powder may cause skin irritation too.

Look for:

- Vomiting and diarrhea
- Mouth and tongue ulcers or inflammation
- Red eyes

1. Rinse the mouth and the eyes with copious amounts of fresh water.
2. Encourage the dog to drink plenty of water. (Do not add salt to food or water to encourage drinking!)
3. Contact your veterinarian for further advice.

Lead

Old lead fishing weights, curtain weights, old lead paint, old pipes and solder, batteries, even old lead toy soldiers are potential sources of lead poisoning for the dog that enjoys chewing.

Look for:

- Initial vomiting, diarrhea and abdominal pain
- Later nervousness and hysteria
- Fear of light, uncoordination
- Staggering, paralysis

1. Induce vomiting if lead has just been eaten.
2. Contact your veterinarian if any of the later signs of lead poisoning have developed. (Blood tests accurately diagnose lead poisoning. Your veterinarian will treat with specific drugs.)

Prevent poisoning:

- Keep all prescription medicines out of the reach of dogs and also where they cannot be knocked down
- Keep all cleaners, garden and do-it-yourself chemicals out of the reach of dogs and where they cannot be knocked down
- Keep all insecticides and petroleum products out of the reach of dogs and where they cannot be knocked down
- When using poisons for weeds, insects or rodents, ensure your dog and other pets cannot get into the areas in which poison has been laid or applied. Follow strictly the instructions on the packet

- When using insecticides directly on a dog, follow strictly the instructions on the packet. Prevent your dog from licking the insecticide off its coat
- Ensure that all medicines, both human and animal, are kept in their original containers and are labelled correctly, including the number of pills originally prescribed. This information will be valuable in case of an accidental overdose

POISONOUS PLANTS

Reduce the risk of accidental poisoning. Prevent your dog from playfully chewing on or eating any of the following plants, flowers or fungi:

- Amaryllis (*Amaryllis*)
- Autumn crocus (*Colochicum autumnale*)
- Bleeding heart (*Dicentra spectabilis*)
- Bloodroot (*Sanguinaria canadensis*)
- Caster oil plant (*Ricinus communis*) (Very dangerous)
- Dumbcane (*Dieffenbachia*) (Very dangerous)
- Flower bulbs of any kind
- Foxglove (*Digitalis purpurea*)
- Jerusalem cherry (*Solanum pseudocapsicum*)
- Larkspur (*Delphinium*)
- Lily of the valley (*Convallaria majalis*)
- Mistletoe (*Viscum album*) (Very poisonous)
- Mushrooms – any wild fungi you cannot safely identify
- Rhubarb (*Rheum rhaponticum*)
- Stinging nettles (*Urtica dioica*)
- Thorn apple or jimsonweed (*Datura stramonium*) (Very dangerous)
- Virginia creeper (*Parthenocissus quinquefolia*)

Do not let your dog chew on leaves, wood or branches from any of these trees or shrubs:

- Azalea
- Box
- Cherry laurel (Very dangerous)
- Chinaberry tree
- Hemlock (Very dangerous)
- Horsechestnut
- Ivy (leaves and berries) (Very dangerous)
- Laburnum
- Oleander (Very dangerous)
- Privet
- Rhododendron
- Wisteria
- Yew (Very dangerous)

PUNCTURE WOUNDS

Puncture wounds to the skin are almost always infected. Bites from other animals may leave little superficial damage but severe problems beneath the skin.

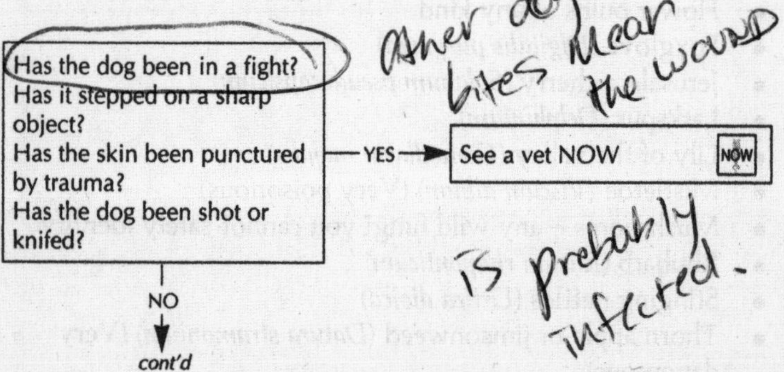
Has the dog been in a fight?
Has it stepped on a sharp object?
Has the skin been punctured by trauma?
Has the dog been shot or knifed?
YES
See a vet NOW
NOW
NO
cont'd

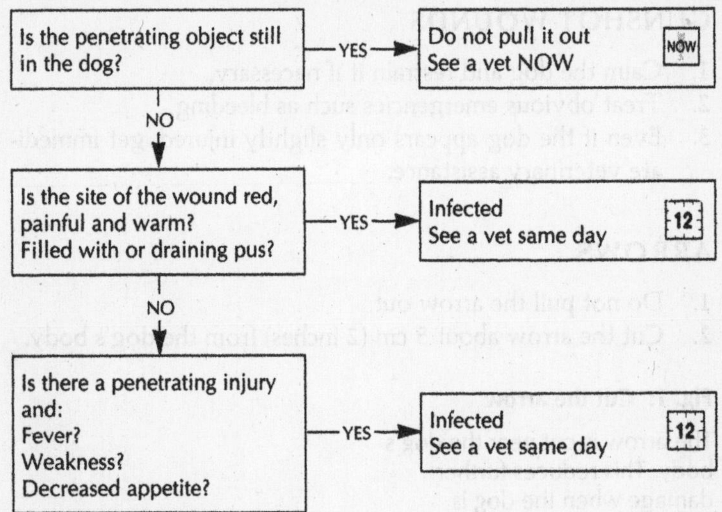

Is the penetrating object still in the dog?
YES
Do not pull it out
See a vet NOW
NOW
NO
Is the site of the wound red, painful and warm?
Filled with or draining pus?
YES
Infected
See a vet same day
12
NO
Is there a penetrating injury and:
Fever?
Weakness?
Decreased appetite?
YES
Infected
See a vet same day
12

ANIMAL BITES

1. Calm the dog. Restrain it and muzzle if necessary. Do not put yourself at risk. The dog might bite you if it is still excited or in pain.
2. If the chest is punctured, cover the wound with a clean, damp cloth. Bandage the chest tightly enough to seal the wound.
3. Monitor shock, give CPR as necessary and get immediate veterinary attention.
4. If the abdomen is punctured and internal organs exposed, prevent the dog from licking or chewing at exposed tissue. When possible, immediately wash any exposed tissue with clean water, wrap the dog's abdomen with a warm, damp sheet, keep the dog warm and get urgent veterinary assistance.
5. If muscle is punctured, clean the wound with 3% hydrogen peroxide, keep the dog warm, monitor for signs of shock and get immediate veterinary help.

Do not use antiseptics or disinfectants on open chest or abdomen puncture wounds.

GUNSHOT WOUNDS

1. Calm the dog and restrain it if necessary.
2. Treat obvious emergencies such as bleeding.
3. Even if the dog appears only slightly injured, get immediate veterinary assistance.

ARROWS

1. Do not pull the arrow out.
2. Cut the arrow about 5 cm (2 inches) from the dog's body.

Fig. 1: Cut the arrow

The arrow is cut near the dog's body. This reduces further damage when the dog is moved.

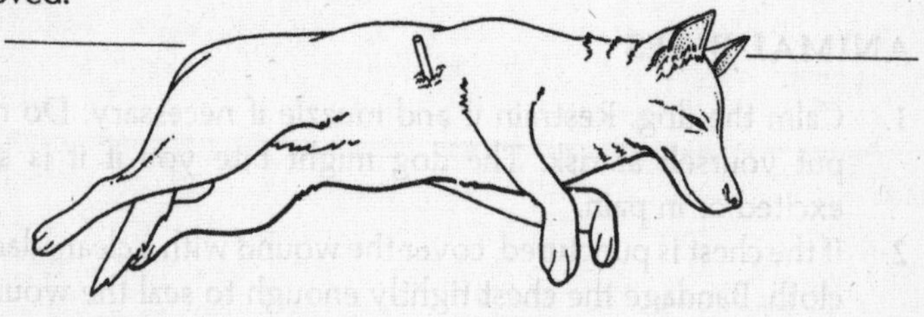

3. Bandage tightly around the arrow's point of entry. (This minimizes movement of the arrow and prevents further internal damage.)
4. Treat shock as necessary and get immediate veterinary attention.

PORCUPINE QUILLS

1. When possible, get immediate veterinary attention. The quills will be removed under anaesthesia.
2. If only a few quills are embedded, use long nosed pliers to pull out each quill following the angle of the quill shaft.

SPLINTERS

1. Wash off dirt and debris from the skin with soap and warm water.
2. Grab the splinter with tweezers and remove it.
3. Once the splinter is removed wash the area again with warm, soapy water or disinfectant.

Do not bandage puncture wounds unless they are bleeding profusely, are in the chest or the penetrating object is still lodged in the wound.

After any penetrating injury always contact your veterinarian. Although tetanus is much less common in dogs than it is in humans, this bacterium thrives in deep wounds. Your veterinarian may want to give tetanus antitoxin.

Tetanus develops five to fifteen days after a penetrating injury. The signs are:

- Sensitivity to light and sound
- Ears stiffer than normal
- Third eyelids protruding
- General stiffness leading to paralysis
- Inability to stand

SCRATCHING

Sudden, intense scratching occurs during allergic reactions. Often called hives, the allergic reaction sometimes leads to dangerous anaphylactic shock. Uncontrolled scratching for other less serious reasons can lead to severe self-inflicted injuries.

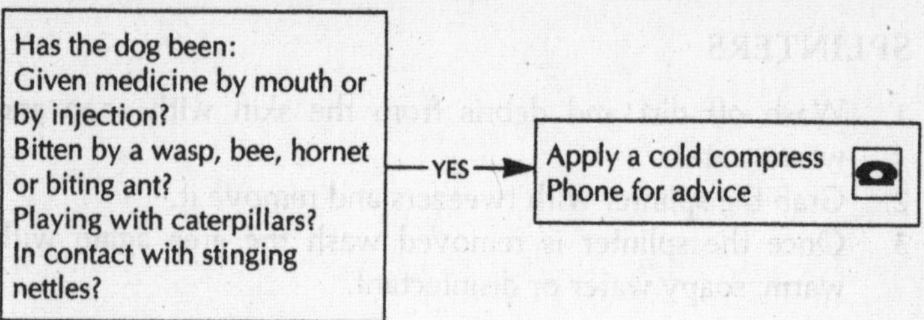
Has the dog been:
Given medicine by mouth or by injection?
Bitten by a wasp, bee, hornet or biting ant?
Playing with caterpillars?
In contact with stinging nettles?
YES
Apply a cold compress
Phone for advice

1. Restrain the dog.
2. Examine the skin and apply cold compresses for fifteen minutes to the most itchy regions.
3. Try to identify and eliminate the cause of itchiness.
4. Give an antihistamine tablet if scratching is intense.
5. If scratching continues or gets worse, make an appointment to see your veterinarian.

Avoid problems:

- When possible, try to prevent your dog from playfully snapping at irritating or biting insects such as wasps
- If a new flea collar is put on the dog, watch carefully for the first few days for signs of local irritation

SWALLOWED OBJECTS

Puppies and inquisitive adult dogs may swallow indigestible articles. Some objects are small enough to pass through the stomach and intestines, while others, such as peach stones, may start the journey but then get stuck. Sometimes, objects remain in the stomach.

WATCH FOR SHOCK

Pale or white gums, rapid breathing, weak and rapid pulse, cold extremities, general weakness.

(For treatment of shock see under **Shock** on page 10.)

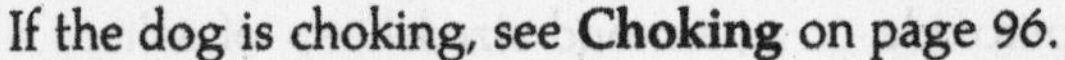
If the dog is choking, see **Choking** on page 96.

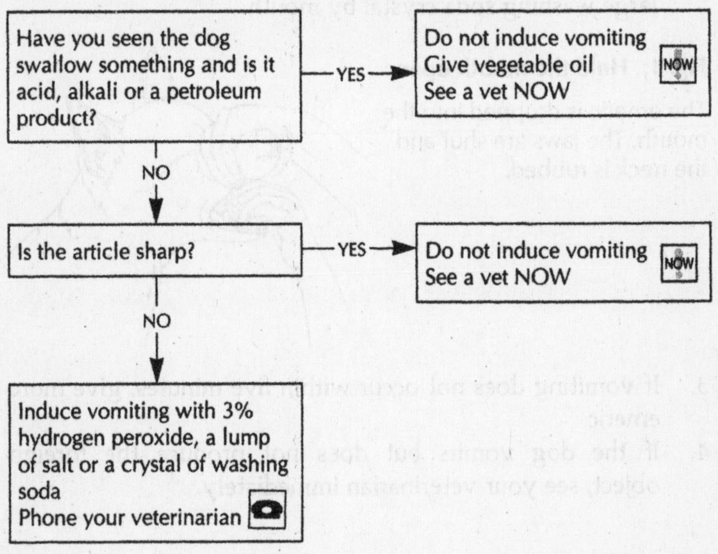
Have you seen the dog swallow something and is it acid, alkali or a petroleum product?
YES
Do not induce vomiting
Give vegetable oil
See a vet NOW
NOW
NO
Is the article sharp?
YES
Do not induce vomiting
See a vet NOW
NOW
NO
Induce vomiting with 3% hydrogen peroxide, a lump of salt or a crystal of washing soda
Phone your veterinarian

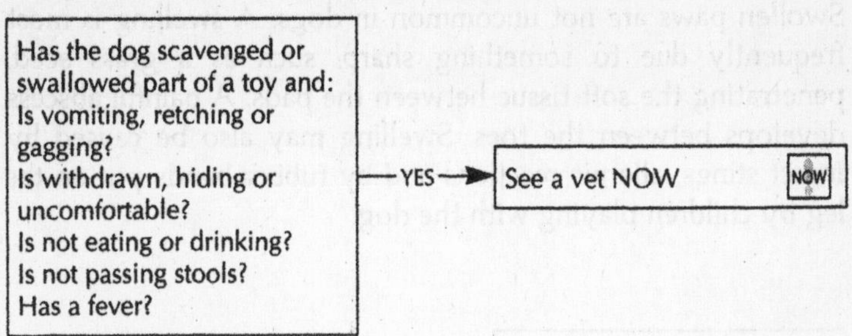
Has the dog scavenged or swallowed part of a toy and:
Is vomiting, retching or gagging?
Is withdrawn, hiding or uncomfortable?
Is not eating or drinking?
Is not passing stools?
Has a fever?
YES
See a vet NOW
NOW

1. If the object is still in the mouth, remove it if possible. Do not pull on thread, string or tinsel hanging from the mouth. Do not cut it short. Get immediate veterinary help.
2. If the object is not alkali, acid, petroleum product or sharp, induce vomiting by giving one to three teaspoons of 3%

hydrogen peroxide or an almond sized lump of salt or a large washing soda crystal by mouth.

Fig. 1: Hold the mouth open

The emetic is dropped into the mouth. The jaws are shut and the neck is rubbed.

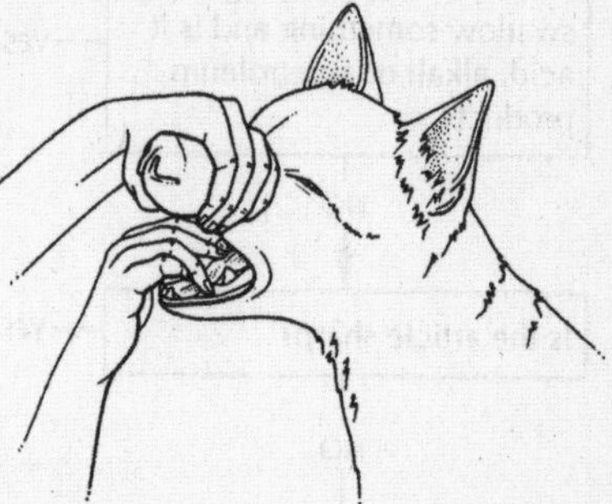

3. If vomiting does not occur within five minutes, give more emetic.
4. If the dog vomits but does not produce the foreign object, see your veterinarian immediately.

SWOLLEN PAWS

Swollen paws are not uncommon in dogs. A swelling is most frequently due to something sharp, such as a grass seed, penetrating the soft tissue between the pads. A painful abscess develops between the toes. Swelling may also be caused by insect stings, allergic reactions and by rubber bands put on the leg by children playing with the dog.

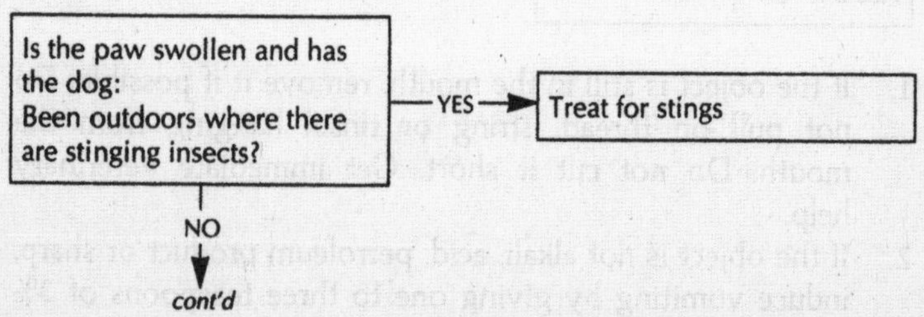
Is the paw swollen and has the dog:
Been outdoors where there are stinging insects?
YES
Treat for stings
NO
cont'd

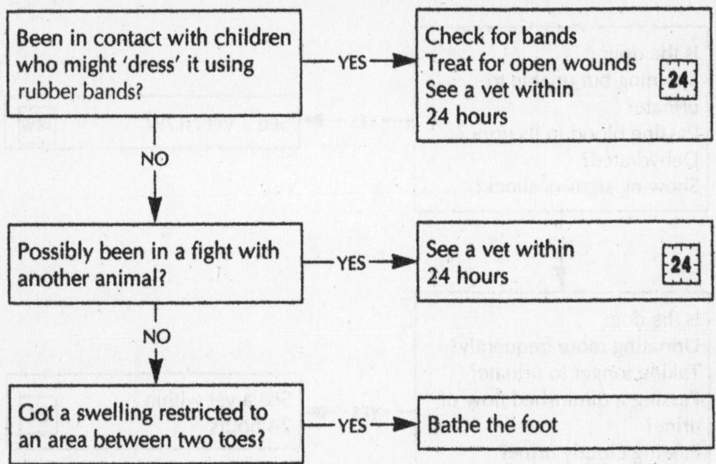
Been in contact with children who might 'dress' it using rubber bands?
YES
Check for bands
Treat for open wounds
See a vet within 24 hours
24
NO
Possibly been in a fight with another animal?
YES
See a vet within 24 hours
24
NO
Got a swelling restricted to an area between two toes?
YES
Bathe the foot

Insect stings are more common in young, playful dogs. Rubber bands may be left on a dog's feet after children have played 'dressing up' with the dog. The elastic rapidly buries itself, especially in dense fur, and can be very difficult to find. Grass seeds are likely to be prevalent at the end of growing seasons.

URINARY PROBLEMS

Anatomically, male dogs are more prone to urinary tract blockages than females. Their prostate glands can enlarge and interfere with urine flow, and bladder stones are more likely to lodge just behind the bone in the penis. Both conditions are very painful.

WATCH FOR SHOCK

Pale or white gums, rapid breathing, weak and rapid pulse, cold extremities, general weakness.

(For treatment of shock see under **Shock** on page 10.)

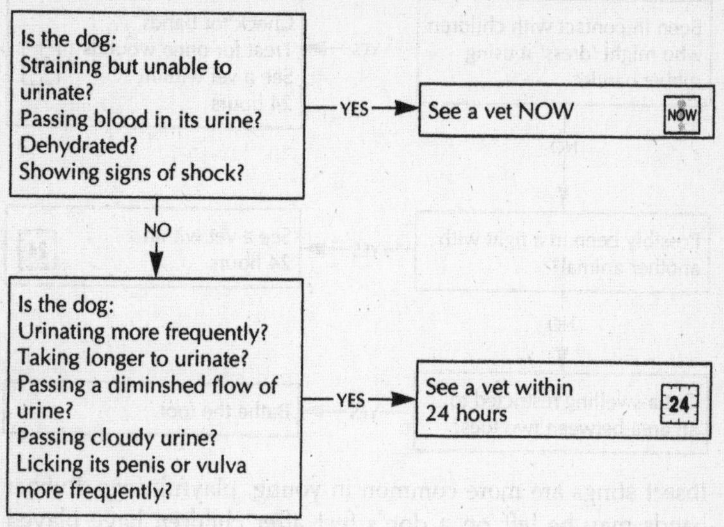
Is the dog:
Straining but unable to urinate?
Passing blood in its urine?
Dehydrated?
Showing signs of shock?
YES
See a vet NOW
NOW
NO
Is the dog:
Urinating more frequently?
Taking longer to urinate?
Passing a diminshed flow of urine?
Passing cloudy urine?
Licking its penis or vulva more frequently?
YES
See a vet within 24 hours
24

If there is a complete blockage:

1. Treat shock if it has developed.
2. Get immediate veterinary assistance.
3. If any urine has been passed, try to collect a sample to help your veterinarian make an accurate diagnosis of the cause of the blockage.

If the dog is passing urine with difficulty:

1. Collect a urine sample in a clean container.
2. See your veterinarian within twenty-four hours.

VOMITING

Drooling, lip licking and excessive swallowing are often signs of nausea and impending vomiting. Dogs readily vomit to empty their stomachs of unwanted material. More serious vomiting accompanies a wide range of serious conditions.

Regurgitation is different from vomiting. Regurgitated brought up fresh and coated with mucus. Regurgitatio sign of esophageal problems.

WATCH FOR SHOCK

Pale or white gums, rapid breathing, weak and rapid pulse, cold extremities, general weakness.

(For treatment of shock see under **Shock** on page 10.)

If vomiting is accompanied by diarrhea see **Diarrhea** on **page 109.**

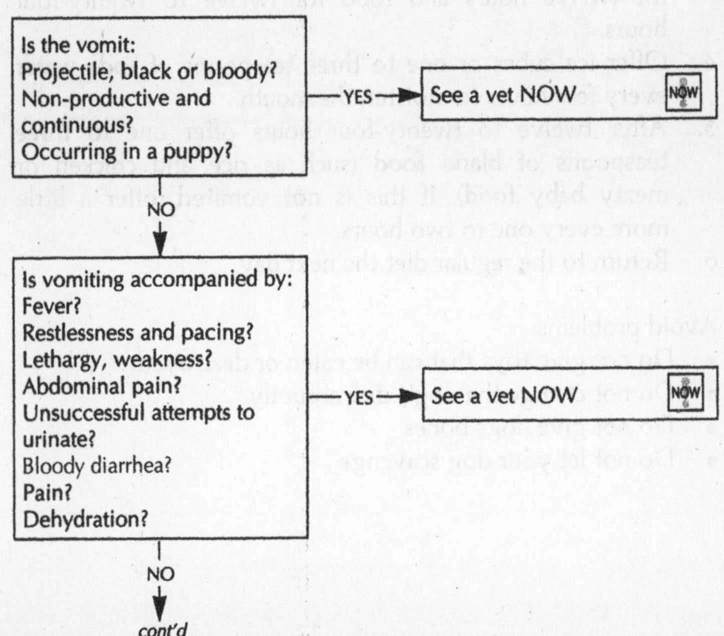
Is the vomit:
Projectile, black or bloody?
Non-productive and continuous?
Occurring in a puppy?
YES
See a vet NOW
NOW
NO
Is vomiting accompanied by:
Fever?
Restlessness and pacing?
Lethargy, weakness?
Abdominal pain?
Unsuccessful attempts to urinate?
Bloody diarrhea?
Pain?
Dehydration?
YES
See a vet NOW
NOW
NO
cont'd

VOMITING

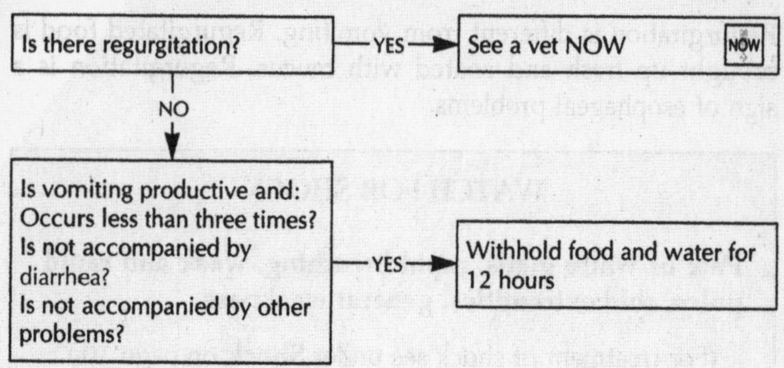

Is there regurgitation?
YES
See a vet NOW
NOW
NO
Is vomiting productive and:
Occurs less than three times?
Is not accompanied by diarrhea?
Is not accompanied by other problems?
YES
Withhold food and water for 12 hours

1. Take away all food and water.
2. If the dog is dehydrated or in shock, treat shock and get immediate veterinary help.
3. If the dog is not dehydrated or in shock, withhold water for twelve hours and food for twelve to twenty-four hours.
4. Offer ice cubes or one to three teaspoons of soda water every few hours to moisten the mouth.
5. After twelve to twenty-four hours offer one to three teaspoons of bland food (such as rice and chicken or meaty baby food). If this is not vomited, offer a little more every one to two hours.
6. Return to the regular diet the next day.

Avoid problems:

- Do not give toys that can be eaten or destroyed
- Do not change the dog's diet abruptly
- Do not give dogs bones
- Do not let your dog scavenge

PART FOUR

PREVENTING EMERGENCIES

How to Reduce the Risk of Emergencies

Reduce the risk of emergencies happening by taking simple precautions:

- Obedience train, control and exercise your dog
  A well trained dog is less prone to accidents. A well exercised dog is less likely to get into serious and dangerous mischief.
- Prevent scavenging
  Secure garbage both inside your home and on your property with tight lids.
- Arrange for a yearly medical examination and booster inoculation
  Prevention or early diagnosis of conditions is almost always physically and financially less costly than emergency treatment.
- Control internal and external parasites
  Parasites spread disease. Worm your dog routinely and control seasonal parasites with appropriate inhibitors and insecticides.
- Neuter your dog
  Discuss neutering with your veterinarian. Neutered dogs are less likely to roam and enjoy reduced risk of several serious medical conditions.

- Provide routine hygienic care for the skin and coat, teeth and gums, nails and anal glands

  Emergencies are less likely to occur if you carry out routine dog 'maintenance'.
- Avoid hazardous household situations

  Keep all household chemicals, cleaners, medicines or dangerous plants out of your dog's reach and in places where they will not fall down. If your dog is a chewer, hide away all electrical cords.
- Avoid hazards when the dog is outdoors

  Never leave a dog in a car on a warm day. Do not let your dog stick its head out of the window of a moving car. Never let a dog travel in the back of a pick-up truck. In cold weather, wash road salt off the dog's paws after exercise.

IDENTIFICATION

Identification is essential in case your dog gets lost. Do not take chances. Permanent identification with tattoos and microchips offers more security than just name tags worn on collars.

TATTOOS

Consider tattooing if there is a standardized identification system where you live. While the dog is sedated a registered number is tattooed inside the ear. Always report your change of address or telephone number to the registering authority.

MICROCHIPS

Consider having an identification microchip implanted under your dog's skin if the dog shelters in your area routinely scan dogs that arrive at the shelters for identifying microchips. The inert microchip contains information that is 'read' when the chip is scanned by a 'reader'. It is inserted by an 'injection' between the shoulders. Always report your change of address or telephone number to the registering authority. (In Europe, all microchips are standardized and readable by different readers.)

ENGRAVED NAME TAGS

Have your dog's name and your telephone number engraved on one side of the tag. Consider having the word 'Vet' and your veterinarian's telephone number engraved on the other side. Replace the tag with a new one when you move home.

NAME CYLINDERS

Write your dog's name and your telephone number on a piece of paper, place it in the cylinder and screw it shut. Cylinders have a tendency to unscrew. Ensure your dog's does not by painting the tightened cylinder with nail varnish. Change the enclosed information when you move home or take your dog on holiday.

TRAINING AND EXERCISE

TRAINING

Training your dog to **sit**, **stay**, **come** and **lie down** is one of the surest ways to reduce the risks of accidents. Of course, with training you also have a more enjoyable companion. Contact your veterinarian for information of the nearest reliable puppy classes or adult dog obedience classes.

EXERCISE

All dogs need physical and mental stimulation. If you must leave your dog at home alone during the day, make sure that it has ample exercise BEFORE you leave. Feed it in the morning rather than when you get home, as this makes it more likely to sleep in your absence. Leave one or two desirable toys for your dog to play with, such as a rawhide bone or a sterilized marrow bone with a little cheese spread or peanut butter pushed well into it. By following this routine it is less likely that your dog will get into mischief and injure itself due to sheer boredom.

VACCINATION

A vaccine stimulates the dog's immune system to build defences against a specific disease. Vaccines are usually made from viruses or bacteria that have been made safe but still stimulate the immune system to create protection. Some vaccines are genetically engineered and contain only the bits of a virus necessary to build immunity. Vaccination has been overwhelmingly successful, for example in virtually eliminating distemper in regions where the majority of dogs are vaccinated.

Your veterinarian will advise on what diseases exist in your area and the prevention program most suitable for your dog.

Diseases commonly vaccinated against include:

Distemper

The signs of distemper are:

- Coughing
- Inflamed and discharging eyes
- Vomiting and diarrhea
- Fever and dehydration

Distemper can be fatal.

Parvovirus

The signs of parvovirus are:

- Severe vomiting and diarrhea possibly with blood

- Lethargy and listlessness
- Dehydration

Parvovirus can be fatal.

Leptospirosis

The signs of Leptospirosis are:

- Lethargy
- Loss of appetite
- Kidney and liver problems

Leptospirosis is transmitted in rat urine and can be contracted while swimming in contaminated water. It can be transmitted to people.

Viral hepatitis

The signs of hepatitis include:

- Vomiting and diarrhea
- Dehydration
- Jaundice

Hepatitis can be fatal.

Parainfluenza

The signs of parainfluenza are:

- Coughing
- Retching
- Loss of appetite

This infection is only mildly debilitating but makes a dog more susceptible to pneumonia.

Bordatella (kennel cough)

The signs of kennel cough are:

- Hacking, dry, non-productive cough
- Gagging
- Copious phlegm production

This infection can be quite debilitating to small or old dogs.

Rabies

Preventative vaccination against rabies is required throughout most of continental Europe and North America. A single vaccination provides protection for between one and three years. Aerial vaccination of foxes throughout both Western and Eastern Europe with genetically engineered anti-rabies vaccine is proving to be an extremely effective measure in reducing and, in some countries, totally eliminating this disease from wildlife.

PARASITE CONTROL

External parasites such as fleas, ticks, mites and lice cause itching but can also transmit a range of diseases. Internal parasites debilitate dogs, increasing the risk of serious conditions developing. Prevent parasites from treating your dog like a mobile restaurant. Follow your veterinarian's advice. Carry out routine parasite prevention measures.

EXTERNAL PARASITES

If your dog has itchy, inflamed or dandruffy skin look for obvious visible parasites. Do not assume there are no parasites if you cannot see any. Most itchy skin problems in dogs are caused by parasites. Make an appointment for your veterinarian to examine your dog.

Prevent parasites from infesting your dog and possibly your family by using insecticides and parasite inhibitors on all your dogs and cats. Always treat your home as well as your dog when fleas are prevalent.

Fleas, ticks, mites, lice

Signs of infestation:

- Itching and scratching

- Inflamed skin
- Dull, dandruffy coat
- Lice eggs glued to hair

Parasites may or may not be visible.

Prevention:

- Start flea prevention before the flea season begins
- Look for ticks after your dog has been in wooded areas
- Do not let your dog share bedding with other animals that have parasites

INTERNAL PARASITES

If your dog has watery or bloody diarrhea, take a stool specimen with you when you visit your veterinarian. Tests can be carried out to determine which internal parasites, if any, are causing the problem.

Roundworm

Signs of infestation:

- Pot belly in pups
- Hiccoughing in pups
- Dull coat
- Poor weight gain or weight loss
- Vomiting or diarrhea, sometimes with pink-white worms passed

Prevention:

- Routinely worm puppies from two weeks of age
- Worm pregnant bitches
- Worm dogs after prolonged treatment with corticosteroids
- In addition, worm all dogs at least twice yearly with medicine recommended by your veterinarian

Tapeworm
Signs of infestation:
- Distended abdomen
- Rice-grain-like egg sacs in fur around anus

Prevention:
- Control fleas on the dog
- Prevent dog from eating animal carcasses and offal
- Worm dog with medicine approved by your veterinarian

Whipworm
Signs of infestation:
- Bloody diarrhea
- Anemia
- Anal irritation and bottom dragging

Prevention:
- Worm dog preventatively
- See your veterinarian if you suspect your dog has whipworms. Special prescription medicines are necessary

Hookworm
Signs of infestation:
- Diarrhea
- Anemia

Prevention:
- Maintain good general hygiene
- See your veterinarian for special prescription medicines if your dog has hookworm

Heartworm
Signs of infestation:
- Gradual weight loss
- Persistent cough
- Reduced capacity to exercise

Prevention:

- Use preventative medicines during the mosquito season

Coccidia, Giardia, Babesia and **Toxoplasma** are other internal parasites for which there is no routine prevention.

BODY CARE

TEETH AND GUMS

If you feed your dog on commercial dog food, dry or moist, or if you give it food from your own table but do not brush or otherwise massage its gums, it will probably develop gum inflammation. By the time the dog's breath smells unpleasant there may be irreversible damage to the roots of some teeth. Keep the teeth and gums healthy and prevent infection.

1. Give high quality rawhide chews. (Rawhide is digestible and needs to be replaced.)
2. Feed proprietary hard snack foods made specifically to exercise the jaws and massage the gums.
3. Ensure that at least part of the dog's diet requires firm chewing.
4. Offer nylon toys that are designed to satisfy a dog's need to chew. (They massage the teeth and gums.)
5. Brush your dog's teeth weekly, using a soft child's toothbrush. (Do not use standard toothpaste, most dogs dislike it. Only use toothpastes formulated specially for dogs. Always reward your dog with praise or a hard snack after you brush its teeth.)
6. If your dog's gums bleed when you brush them, they are already inflamed. Make an appointment to see your veterinarian.

Never give a dog soft poultry bones. They splinter, are easily swallowed and can lodge in the intestines. They can also cause painful constipation.

Give hard beef marrow bones only under supervision. Beef bones can only be crushed by the strongest jaws. Gnawing on beef marrow bones is a good way to ensure healthy teeth and gums, but there is always a risk that a tooth might be fractured in the process.

NAILS

The tips of a dog's nails should touch but not scrape on the ground. Small dogs need their nails cut more frequently than large or heavy dogs.

1. Hold the paw and look for the living pink tissue (the quick) inside.

Fig. 1: Cutting the nails

(a) How to cut a dog's nails

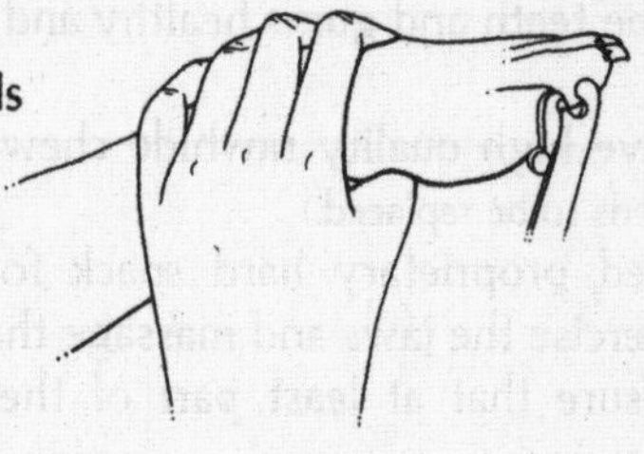

(b) Where to cut the nail

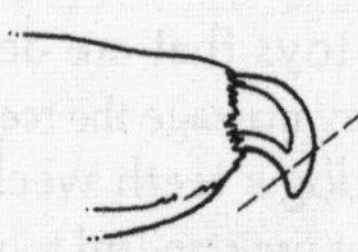

2. Using purpose made dog nail clippers cut the nail just in front of the quick.
3. If the quick bleeds, apply pressure for two minutes to the cut end of the nail with an absorbent pad. (Cut your dog's nails just after it has been bathed, when the nails are softer and more pliant.)

4. If your dog has black nails, ask your veterinarian to cut them to reduce the risk of damaging the sensitive quick.

ANAL SACS

If your dog is scraping or dragging its bottom along the ground (or worse, on the carpet) it may have blocked anal scent glands.

The signs of blocked glands are:

- Scooting
- Dragging
- Rubbing
- Licking the anal region
- Licking the groin or hind legs
- Suddenly jumping up and looking at the hind quarters

Blocked anal glands should be emptied. Your veterinarian can show you how to do it. Preventative emptying reduces the risk of a painful anal abscess forming.

SKIN AND HAIR

Groom your dog routinely according to the specific needs of its coat type. Prevent fleas or treat them at the first sign of their presence. Fleas account for perhaps three out of every four skin problems seen by veterinarians.

1. Brush your dog daily. (Brushing prevents matting but also removes dead hair and loosens dry flaking skin, preventing it from building up. Brushing allows you to examine your dog thoroughly. It should be an enjoyable experience for you and your dog. An added bonus is that brushing your dog reinforces that you are the boss.)
2. Bathe your dog as frequently or infrequently as necessary. (Follow your veterinarian's advice. Some dogs need baths only

twice yearly, while others need weekly washes. Only use shampoos designed for use on dog hair unless advised otherwise.)

3. Do not use dietary supplements in excess. (Sunflower oil and corn oil at a dose of between one and three teaspoons a day, or proprietary 'GLA' oil supplements may improve a very dry skin if given for at least a month.)

DIET

Good nutrition is essential for good health. Make sure your dog always has access to fresh water. Feed a well balanced diet that is appropriate for your dog's age, condition and energy level.

1. Feed commercial foods only from reputable manufacturers.
2. Ensure that eating exercises your dog's teeth and gums.
3. Serve food at room or body temperature, not directly out of the refrigerator.
4. Discard any dry food not eaten in twenty-four hours.
5. Discard any moist food not eaten in one hour.
6. Make sure a bowl of fresh water is always available.

- Do not feed dogs with cat food (It is too rich in protein)
- Never feed food that is stale or spoiled
- Never feed brittle bones
- Do not let your dog get overweight

Weigh your dog accurately every month. Creeping weight gain can be detected early and nipped in the bud. Weight loss, detected early, can be a sign of illness or disease.

WEIGHT WATCHING

Use this chart as a very rough guide to the dietary requirements of different sized dogs and how many kilocalories you should feed to ensure weight loss. True requirements vary according to the age and energy level of the dog and the climate in which it lives.

Target weight (Kg)	*(lbs)*	*Normal carlorie requirement (Kilocalories)*	*Dieting requirement (Kilocalories)*
2.5	5.5	250	150
5	11	450	270
10	22	750	450
15	33	1000	600
20	44	1250	750
25	55	1500	900
30	66	1700	1000
35	77	1880	1150
40	88	2100	1250
45	99	2300	1400
50	110	2500	1500
55	121	2600	1600
60	132	2700	1700

You should be able to feel your dog's ribs. If you cannot, your dog is probably overweight. Reduce calorie intake, not the frequency of meals. Feeding a fat dog a calorie reduced diet, little and often, satisfies the dog's desire to eat constantly. This reduces begging and scavenging.

NEUTERING

Neutering does not make a dog less playful. It does not diminish a dog's ability to guard. What it DOES do is make sex a less important item on the dog's agenda. And when sex is less important, accidents are less likely. As an added benefit females are less likely to develop mammary tumors and males are less likely to develop prostate problems.

The advantages of neutering males dogs include:

- Less aggression towards other male dogs
- Less wandering
- Less urine marking
- Less likelihood of developing prostate problems
- No testicular tumors
- Easier to train
- No fathering of unwanted litters

The disadvantages of neutering male dogs include:

- Inability to father litters in the future
- A tendency to gain weight (Weight gain is experienced by ten per cent of dogs after they are neutered. Excess weight is readily controlled by adjusting the dog's diet)

The advantages of neutering female dogs include:

- No unwanted pregnancies
- No twice-yearly heat cycle and bleeding
- No twice-yearly hormonally induced mood changes
- Less risk of mammary tumors (The risk drops to zero if the female is neutered before her first season)
- No risk of life threatening womb infection (pyometra) later in life (Pyometra is a common emergency in older females. Immediate surgery to remove the pus filled womb is necessary)

The disadvantages of neutering female dogs include:

- Inability to have puppies
- A tendency to gain weight (Weight gain is experienced by ten per cent of dogs after they are neutered. Excess weight is readily controlled by adjusting the dog's diet)

HOW TO GIVE ORAL MEDICINES

Few dogs accept being forced to swallow medicines willingly. Be firm but gentle. Always reward your dog afterwards with soothing words and strokes. When possible, hide the medicine or associate it with something the dog finds enjoyable.

Pills:

1. Calm the dog by speaking to it soothingly. Tell it to sit with its back against the wall. A small dog can be placed on a table.
2. With your forefinger and thumb just behind the canine teeth, draw the jaw up and the upper lips down.
3. Tilt the dog's head back.
4. With the pill in your other hand, draw the lower jaw down and drop or place the pill as far back over the tongue as possible.

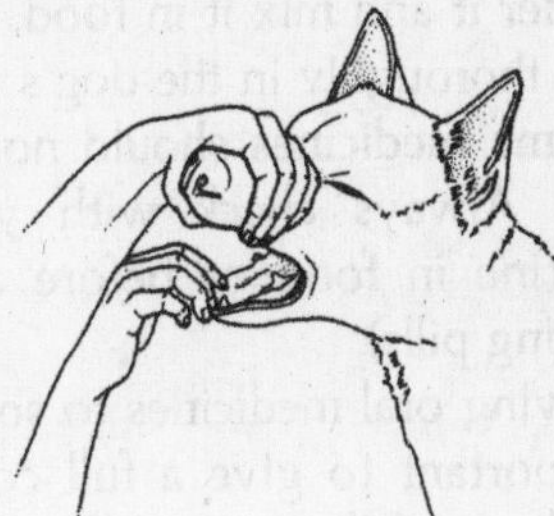

Fig. 1: Drop or place the pill in the mouth

Hold the head up to reduce the risk of the pill being spat out.

5. Close the dog's mouth immediately and rub its throat until you see the dog swallow.

Fig. 2: Rub the throat

This stimulates swallowing.

6. Open the mouth to make sure the pill has been swallowed. If it has, praise the dog. If not, repeat the exercise.

Liquid medicines:

1. Hold the upper jaw as you would when giving a pill.
2. Keep the head level. Do not tilt it back as you would when giving a pill.
3. Tip or squirt the medicine into the side of the mouth. Do not squirt it in the back of the mouth, as it might go down the windpipe.
4. Close the mouth and rub the throat until the dog swallows.
5. Praise the dog.

Whenever possible, hide pills in food such as a ball of bread, cheese or peanut butter. Alternatively, if the pill is tasteless, powder it and mix it in food. Hide liquid medicines by mixing them thoroughly in the dog's favorite food.

Some medicines should not be given with certain types of food. Always check with your veterinarian before hiding medicine in food or before altering it in any way (such as crushing pills).

Giving oral medicines to some dogs is extremely difficult. It is important to give a full course of prescribed medicines. If you have difficulties, contact your veterinarian. If you are bitten, always seek medical advice.

HOW TO GIVE EYE MEDICINES

Make certain that eye drops, lotions or ointments come into direct contact with the eye itself.

Eye ointment:

1. Speak calmly to the dog and tell it to sit where it cannot back away. Put a small dog on a table.

2. Clean away any eye discharge with a piece of cotton wool dampened with tepid or warm water.
3. With the thumb of one hand, draw the lower lid down. (This forms a space for the ointment.)
4. Support the other hand holding the eye ointment against the dog's head. (This prevents the ointment container from hitting the eye if the dog moves abruptly.)
5. Squeeze a line of ointment in the space formed between the lower lid and the eyeball.(Ointment runs more smoothly if the tube is first warmed in your hands.)

Fig. 1: Squeeze the ointment into the eye

The hand holding the ointment is steadied against the dog's head.

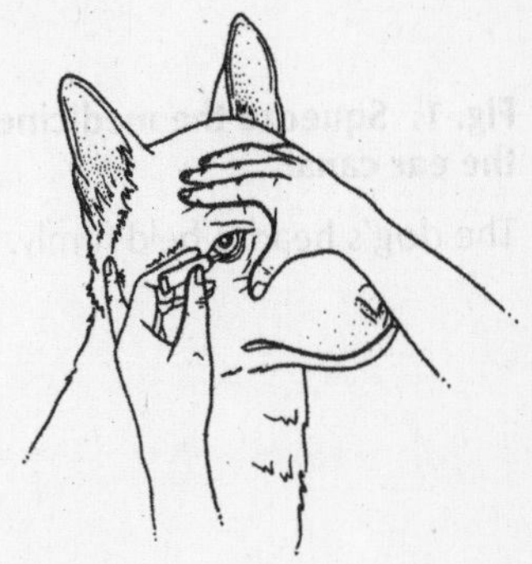

6. Close the eye. (This spreads the ointment evenly over the eye and throughout the socket. Cold ointments often appear grey/white but with body heat become clear within minutes.)
7. Praise the dog and give it a food reward.

Eye drops:

1. Follow the above instructions but do not draw the lower lid away.
2. Squeeze an eye drop on to the upper part of the eye.

Always take care that the medicine container does not come into contact with the eye.

HOW TO GIVE EAR MEDICINES

To be effective, ear medicines should reach right down to the eardrum. Most bottles and tubes come with applicator nozzles large enough to fit the ear but not so large that they cause damage.

1. Restrain the dog and command it to sit.
2. Hold the ear (or lift the ear of lop-eared dogs) with one hand and insert the nozzle of the ear medicine into the opening to the ear canal with the other.
3. Squeeze the tube or bottle.

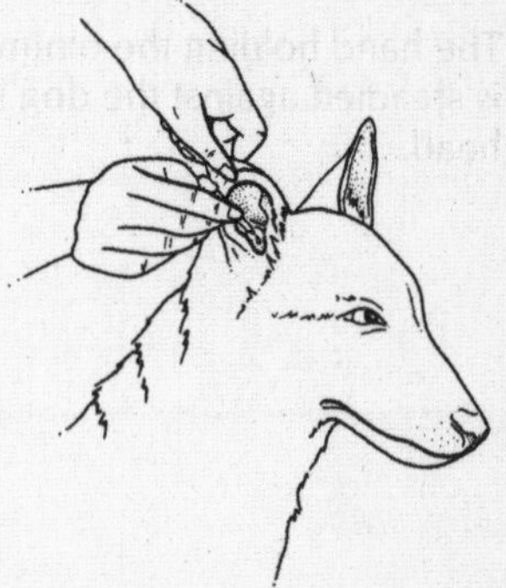

Fig. 1: Squeeze the medicine into the ear canal

The dog's head is held firmly.

4. Drop the ear back into place and massage the ear canal. (A squelching sound means the medicine is being thoroughly massaged in the canal.)

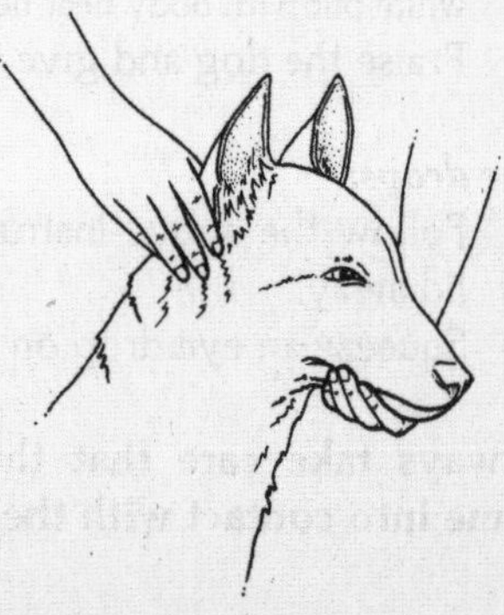

Fig. 2: Massage the ear canal

Rub the area below the point where the ear meets the head.

5. Hold the ear flap and swab away excess medicine and debris. (This prevents medicine from flying everywhere when the dog then shakes its head.)
6. Praise the dog and give it a food reward.

Never use proprietary wax removers if there is a risk that the eardrum has been ruptured.

HOW TO GIVE INJECTIONS

Insulin injections are usually needed to treat sugar diabetes, but your veterinarian might provide you with life saving medicine to give by injection if your dog is known to go into anaphylactic shock when bitten by wasps or other insects. Giving injections sounds daunting but is quite simple, simpler in many ways than giving medicines by mouth.

1. Draw the medicine into the syringe.
2. Tap air bubbles until they rise to the top of the syringe then expel them until the first drop of medicine emerges from the needle.
3. Tell the dog to stay.
4. While speaking calmly to the dog, grasp a fold of skin on the neck between the shoulder blades. (This is a relatively insensitive part of the skin.)
5. With a steady movement, insert the needle through the skin into the tissue under the skin and above underlying muscle, then squeeze the contents of the syringe into that space. (Alternatively, your veterinarian may instruct you to give certain life saving drugs directly into the muscles of the hind leg. Follow those instructions carefully.)
6. Praise the dog for obedience and give a food reward.

FIRST AID KIT

It is easy and simple to prepare a first aid kit for dog emergencies. Keep one in the car and another at home. Remember to keep the kit out of the reach of small children.

Bandage material:
- Sterile non-stick gauze pads 7.5 × 7.5 cm (3 × 3 inches)
- Gauze bandage 2.5 and 5 cm (1 and 2 inch) rolls
- Elastic adhesive tape 2.5 and 5 cm (1 and 2 inch) rolls
- Blunt-tipped scissors

Cleaning material:
- Cotton buds
- Absorbent cotton wool
- 3% Hydrogen peroxide
- Tweezers

Other essential items:
- Thermometer
- Sticks for splints (tongue depressors)

Other useful items:
- Needle-nosed pliers
- 1 metre (3 feet) soft nylon rope for muzzle or emergency leash
- Blanket

PHARMACY

Allergy or itchiness:
- Antihistamine tablets or liquid – follow instructions for children

Coughs:
- Glyceryl guiacolate expectorant – 2–5 ml every four

hours. (Use a cough suppressant only under the advice and supervision of your veterinarian.)

Diarrhoea:

- Kaopectate – 5 ml per 5 Kg (10 lbs) body weight every four hours for one day

Poisoning:

- Activated charcoal (one teaspoon of a suspension for dogs under 10 Kg (25 lbs) and two teaspoons for dogs over that weight)
- 3% Hydrogen peroxide (one to two teaspoons every ten minutes until vomiting is induced)
- Vegetable oil (one to two teaspoons for dogs under 10 Kg (25 lbs) and one to two tablespoons for dogs over that weight)

Index

Page numbers in *italic* refer to the illustrations

Index

FOR THE BEST IN PAPERBACKS, LOOK FOR THE 

In every corner of the world, on every subject under the sun, Penguin represents quality and variety—the very best in publishing today.

For complete information about books available from Penguin—including Penguin Classics, Penguin Compass, and Puffins—and how to order them, write to us at the appropriate address below. Please note that for copyright reasons the selection of books varies from country to country.

In the United States: Please write to *Penguin Group (USA), P.O. Box 12289 Dept. B, Newark, New Jersey 07101-5289* or call 1-800-788-6262.

In the United Kingdom: Please write to *Dept. EP, Penguin Books Ltd, Bath Road, Harmondsworth, West Drayton, Middlesex UB7 0DA.*

In Canada: Please write to *Penguin Books Canada Ltd, 90 Eglinton Avenue East, Suite 700, Toronto, Ontario M4P 2Y3.*

In Australia: Please write to *Penguin Books Australia Ltd, P.O. Box 257, Ringwood, Victoria 3134.*

In New Zealand: Please write to *Penguin Books (NZ) Ltd, Private Bag 102902, North Shore Mail Centre, Auckland 10.*

In India: Please write to *Penguin Books India Pvt Ltd, 11 Panchsheel Shopping Centre, Panchsheel Park, New Delhi 110 017.*

In the Netherlands: Please write to *Penguin Books Netherlands bv, Postbus 3507, NL-1001 AH Amsterdam.*

In Germany: Please write to *Penguin Books Deutschland GmbH, Metzlerstrasse 26, 60594 Frankfurt am Main.*

In Spain: Please write to *Penguin Books S. A., Bravo Murillo 19, 1° B, 28015 Madrid.*

In Italy: Please write to *Penguin Italia s.r.l., Via Benedetto Croce 2, 20094 Corsico, Milano.*

In France: Please write to *Penguin France, Le Carré Wilson, 62 rue Benjamin Baillaud, 31500 Toulouse.*

In Japan: Please write to *Penguin Books Japan Ltd, Kaneko Building, 2-3-25 Koraku, Bunkyo-Ku, Tokyo 112.*

In South Africa: Please write to *Penguin Books South Africa (Pty) Ltd, Private Bag X14, Parkview, 2122 Johannesburg.*

PO #: 4500306593